The Great 38th

Passes House by 19 Votes
With Other Levies Reduced

Jam-Packed Galleries Listen to Sales Tax Debate

Senate Backs Early Ballot

JOHN CORLETT

The GREAT 38*th*

The 1965 Idaho Legislature and the making of a perfect political storm

Chas. McDevitt

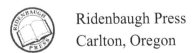

Ridenbaugh Press
Carlton, Oregon

THE GREAT 38th: The 1965 Idaho Legislature and the Making of a Perfect Political Storm

Copyright ©2022 by Chas. McDevitt

For more information, contact Ridenbaugh Press, P.O. Box 834, Carlton OR 97111.

Printed and bound in the United States of America.

First edition January 2022

10 9 8 7 6 5 4 3 2 1

Library of Congress Cataloging in Publication Data

Chas. McDevitt

The '65 Session

Bibliography

1. History. 2. Idaho Politics and Government.

I. McDevitt, Chas. II. Title.

ISBN 978-0-945648-53-6 (softbound)

Ridenbaugh Press
P.O. Box 834, Carlton OR 97111
Phone (503) 852-0010
www.ridenbaugh.com
stapilus@ridenbaugh.com

Contents

The content of this book was completed by the author, Chuck McDevitt, three weeks before his death on May 29, 2021. It was finalized by Idaho political consultant Sal Celeski and Ridenbaugh publisher Randy Stapilus.

This book is dedicated to the 123 members of the 38th Idaho Legislature and their state support personnel, who created the historic achievements of the 1965 legislature for the ongoing benefit of the people of the state of Idaho.

Senator Says He'd Ask Sales Tax Repeal

BOISE (AP) — Sen. Don G. Fredericksen, D-Gooding, said Saturday that if the 1965 Idaho Legislature approves a sales tax he will lead a campaign to repeal it by initiative procedure.

The method was used 30 years ago to repeal a 2 per cent sales tax enacted by the legislature. Repeal came at the first general election after the law became effective.

"If we can't control it some other way," Fredericksen said of the sales tax, "let's give the people a chance to decide on it."

⬛ ⬛

BROTHERLY FOES — Members of the Idaho House of Representatives include two brothers, Rep. Charles McDevitt, left, of Ada County, and Rep. Herman McDevitt of Bannock County. But they sit on opposite sides of the House aisle, where they posed for this picture. Charles is a Republican and his brother is a Democrat. (AP Wirephoto)

Acknowledgements

Over the years news articles, editorials, memos, biographies, autobiographies, and political columns have alluded to, referenced, or summarized events and actions of the 37th and 38th Sessions of the Idaho legislature. I continued to wait for someone to do a little more in-depth writing about what, why, and by whom these sessions had accomplished such a record of dynamic change.

As the years passed, more and more of the players in the 37th and 38th Sessions passed on. With the loss of each of these individuals, part of the story was lost. I finally concluded that I must attempt to chronicle, as best I could, the untold tale of how and why what was done—and to fully recognize the individuals who actually made the accomplishments of those years possible.

I really had no idea of what I had undertaken.

In order to place the tax situation of Idaho in the 1960s in context, tax efforts of earlier years had to be understood. Bill Crookham of Caldwell made available all of the papers, letters, and records of George Crookham's decade-long attempts to modernize the tax system. Susan Stacy reviewed, analyzed, and selectively copied hundreds of pages of newspapers from the period of 1962 through 1966 in order to capture the political impact of these legislative sessions as it played out in the media. The volumes of session laws of 1963 and 1965 became dog-eared, as they, as well as the *Journals* of the House and Senate, were visited again and again to strive for accuracy.

For months on end my wife, Virginia, tolerated tables loaded with news stories, legislative journals, session laws, private letters, notes, drafts of bills, and drafts of my efforts, which she also proofread while reminding me from time to time that the effort was not yet finished.

This account could not have been properly related without the inclusion of pictorial reproduction of the people and events that created it. And, that could only have been possible with the resources of the Idaho State Archives and the dedicated assistance of staff members; Danielle Grundel, HannaLore Hein, Angie K. Davis, and especially retired historian/editor Judy Austin.

Research assistance securing photographs; Boise State University Library / Special Collections Personnel; Alessandro Meregaglia and Gwyn Hervochon, Freda Cenarrusa, Roy Eiguren, George Crookham, Murriah Clifton, Ernie Hoidal and Scott Simplot and the J.R. Simplot Company.

In addition, the *Idaho Statesman* (Boise) and the *Lewiston Tribune* made their historical archives available for use. Those combined resources provided the added dimension that helped to bring all the words and the history back to life.

Sal Celeski, former reporter and former news director of KTVB Channel 7, attended almost every day of the legislative sessions and was always available to answer questions, provide insights, or add interest to often-boring sentences of the author.

Darrell Manning, Minority Leader during the 37th and 38th Sessions, reviewed drafts, provided insights from his vantage point, and made valuable suggestions of issues to be addressed.

Heather Houle had for more than a decade maintained our law office in a high level of efficiency and productivity. On closing the office, Heather volunteered to assist in any way the anticipated completion of this undertaking. Months turned into years and draft after draft of restructuring and editing; Heather persisted throughout; without her, this effort probably would never have come to a close.

4

To all of the above individuals I express my utmost appreciation and thanks. I hope that this effort will assist in an understanding of just how the gains made in 1963 and 1965 were possible.

Twenty years ago . . .

this is how The Statesman assessed the 38th Idaho Legislature.

Record State Expenditure Challenges Educators, Elected Officials to Rebuild, Improve Services

The record biennium budget set by the 38th session of the Idaho Legislature begins what many suggest is a "new day" for the state, especially in the field of education and the improvement of state services.

The challenge now before the state's servants, from Gov. Robert E. Smylie on down, is to spend this record sum wisely and see that effective improvements are brought about, that educational deficiencies be corrected.

The goal of the state's educational leaders has not been reached merely by providing teachers with more pay. The generosity of the Idaho Legislature signals educators to take the ball and show how they can start rebuilding the ranks of their own profession and the processes of learning to meet the needs of today and the future.

* * * *

An equitable formula for state aid to education may someday come to pass since the legislature took the heroic step of establishing a centralized office to reclassify property tax assessments on a statewide basis within a period of four years.

The inequities in the state's past property assessments can now be eased through the 20 per cent formula for assessing real and personal property and 40 per cent on utilities.

* * * *

In Ada County, for example, the owner of a $10,000 home will be assessed under the 20-20-40 formula at 20 per cent of its full cash value, a figure of $2,000.

Under the new law, the provision that the assessed valuation be increased also requires that the levy be decreased, and that no additional taxes be imposed because of uniform assessments.

Statewide, the tax on a $10,000 residential property now averages $129, but under the formula the tax would be $150.

In Ada County, the tax on a $10,000 home averages now $157, compared to $183 under the formula. In Boise, the same house carries an average $179 property tax, compared to $211 when the formula goes into effect.

The 1964 assessed valuation of Idaho is $760,688,541. Under the new tax formula, the assessed valuation would increase within four years to an estimated total of $1,039,986,470.

The average levy statewide on each $100 assessed valuation is now $10.28. Under the new program the levy would be reduced in four years' time to $7.52.

On that $10,000 home in Ada County,

the owner is now paying on the average of $12.56 per $100. Under the new formula the same owner will pay $9.13 per $100.

In other words, the assessed valuation goes up, but the levy comes down, resulting in the tax increase of $26.

The Boise levy averages now $14.35 per $100, compared to $10.56 under the new formula.

Under the equalization bill, commercial buildings receive some relief, utilities will pay nearly the same, according to some accountants, but more, say others, under the 40 per cent factor.

Schools fared sumptuously, with the final general fund appropriation of $57.3 million in state aid, a biennium increase of $17.3 million.

District school trustees can now levy from the present 30-mill maximum to 40 mills for maintenance and operation, or a potential statewide increase load of nearly $16 million. Most observers believe that many districts will go to the 35-mill limit, but few will set the 40-mills.

However, the property relief in ad valorem taxes, teachers' retirement levy and education Social Security absorbed by the sales tax revenue can be offset if the school district hikes to a maximum 40-mill levy for maintenance and operations.

The sales tax cares for the $17 million increase in state aid to education. Districts can now reduce levies on basis. Will they?

* * * *

The 38th lawmaking session was progressive. It was in a mood to spend. More so the legislators wanted to catch up with their past omissions and escapes.

The leadership of the governor was bold, and generally received bipartisan acceptance.

How will this new executive and legislative boldness be interpreted by the majority of Idahoans, by the many varied business and agricultural interests, the officials of the county and local governments?

Shall we move ahead, or turn back? Shall we meet our obligations or do we prefer to retreat from them?

State officials, particularly the politicians, will watch carefully. The taxpayers aren't asleep. The voters will view their state government in action. They'll keep an eye on education with more interest than ever before.

The "greatness" of the 38th legislature will be judged by the people. All told, The Statesman believes the public generally will abide by the decisions of their representatives. But it often is difficult to change and to move ahead.

38th Session,
Idaho State Legislature

On March 18, 1965, after 73 days, the words "adjourned sine die" brought to a simple end what would ultimately be widely regarded as the most productive legislative session in Idaho history.

With this pronouncement by Pete Cenarrusa, Speaker of the Idaho House of Representatives, in the House Chamber and the similar declaration by W. E. (Bill) Drevlow, Lieutenant Governor, in the Senate Chamber, the regular Session of the 38th Idaho Legislature (1965) was ended. The successes and failures of the 38th Session contained in the records of the state would be judged and fully recognized with the passage of time.

The 38th-Session legislators did not have to wait long for the judgments to begin to be rendered.

On March 19, Boise's *Idaho Daily Statesman* quoted Governor Robert E. Smylie describing the 38th Session as "one of the greatest, if not the greatest session in Idaho's history." This assessment by the governor was followed quickly by similar editorials in the *Idaho Daily Statesman*, the *Lewiston Morning Tribune*, the *Twin Falls Times-News*, the Pocatello *Idaho State Journal*, and almost all the major publications in the state.

John Corlett of the *Idaho Daily Statesman*, the dean of state political columnists who chronicled legislative activities for decades, analyzed the 38th Idaho Legislature as follows: "one of the best in the State's history as it puts Idaho on the road to growth and greatness and the recrimination of the moment will have no part in the historic valuation of the session of 1965."

The assessments continued; when, uncharacteristically, members of the 38th Legislature held a 20-year reunion in 1985, the *Lewiston Morning Tribune* published an editorial with the headline "Oh for another Legislature like that one," extolling the accomplishments of the 38th Session.

Who were the people comprising the Legislature in 1965? What had they accomplished? Why was their action so acclaimed? What were the unique dynamics that made their exceptional actions possible?

The political climate

Beginning in 1945 with the return of thousands of soldiers to Idaho, the impact of their raising families and the start of the "baby boom," it became apparent that Idaho's tax structure was not capable of supporting the services demanded by the voting public.

Various workable solutions to a tax structure that relied almost totally on real property tax and income tax were discussed without significant progress. Idaho's real property tax had become one of the highest in the nation. Both corporate and personal income taxes were at a level that did not allow for significant increase, as the federal government had preempted the income-tax field at an ever increasing rate. In 1955, House Bill (HB) 334 established a committee, its members to be appointed by the governor, to do a thorough and complete study of the tax structure of the state. Two members each were appointed from the House and from the Senate, one from each party. The remaining members were selected from all segments of the economy of the state. The committee sought input through statewide hearings and returned its report to Governor Smylie on November 15, 1956.

The committee's report reviewed the Idaho economy from 1945 to 1947 and from 1955 to 1957, examining the tax structure and the need for major tax revision—including revision of real property tax, income tax, and distribution of funds to municipalities and counties as well as revision of the taxing authority available to local school districts.

The report declared that "it is the unanimous conclusion of the Committee that the present tax structure is inadequate. It is neither feasible nor equitable to secure substantial necessary revenue from a higher Income Tax or a higher Property Tax, the then two major current sources of revenue...."

The committee proposed major tax reform, including enacting a sales tax and distribution of certain sources of general funds and specific tax yields. The 34th Session (1957) of the legislature reviewed the report, which had been transmitted (without recommendation) to it by the governor. As a result, HB 203, establishing a 2-percent sales tax and containing some tax reform, was passed in the House of Representatives by a 42-to-15 vote.

However, when it was transmitted to the Senate, it was assigned to a committee that ensured it never saw the light of day. As a result of the 1958 general election, Democrats won control of the legislature as well as every statewide elective office save that of governor: Republican Bob Smylie retained that position.

The 1959 Democrat-controlled legislature added a ten-dollar surcharge to every income tax return, which promptly became known as the "head tax." The head tax was widely disliked by Idaho voters. During the 1960 general election campaign, Republican candidates held up the head tax as a despicable piece of legislation and vowed to repeal it. Democrats arrived at the same conclusion, but they lost control of both houses of the legislature.

Governor Smylie's budget message to the 1961 Legislature proposed keeping the head tax but dedicating it to financing a permanent building fund. Democrats lacked the votes to address repeal, so the head tax remained.

The Democrats thought that the governor and Republican legislators had not kept faith with them by refusing to permit a vote on a bill repealing the head tax, which the Democrats could have voted for in order to keep their campaign promises.

This resulted in rancor that permeated all legislative action in the 1961 Session.

Pete T. Cenarrusa-Speaker-Blaine

In the organization of the Republican-controlled House of Representatives in 1963 (37th Session), Pete T. Cenarrusa (a rancher from Carey, Blaine County) was elected Speaker of the House.

Cenarrusa was a quiet, soft-spoken man, non-confrontational, personable, and easy to talk with. His nature did not, however, suggest a man who could be detached from his principles.

W. J. Lanting-Twin Falls

At the same time William J. (Bill) Lanting, a farmer from Hollister, just south of Twin Falls, was elected Majority Leader of the House. Like Cenarrusa, Lanting was relatively quiet, handled himself extremely well on the floor of the House, and—also like Cenarrusa—was not a person to be taken lightly.

At the same time Darrell Manning (Bannock) was elected House Minority Leader. Manning, an Air Force pilot, was one who would seek accommodation, if possible, without giving up any fundamental principles.

D. V. Manning-Bannock

Manning was extremely thorough and possessed, to my knowledge, the only complete copy of Cannon's Rules in Idaho. It contained the official procedural rules of the United States House of Representatives and was relied on, along with Robert's Rules of Order, as fundamental principles of procedure by many state legislative bodies.

As a result of these individuals and their leadership positions, the 1963 Session appeared to meet in a spirit of good will despite the bitterness that had prevailed in the 1961 Session. This favorable spirit continued to nurture and grow in the 1965 (38th) Session.

The unique dynamics

Many of the issues that were tackled by the 38th Idaho Legislature had perplexed the state as serious needs for a number of years. They had escaped a solution because of increased political rancor and diminishing support from a fiscal tax structure that no longer was able to answer the growing demand for increasing state services.

In addition, the legislature was faced with a court-mandated "One Man, One Vote" reapportionment edict in order to comply with the interpretation of the United States Constitution as then being applied by the United States Supreme Court. This meant that in effect the 1965 legislators would not be returning to the legislative districts that they had been elected to represent.

The boundaries of all legislative districts would be redrawn to conform to equal population representation. Legislators were facing the loss of their political jobs based on the action that they themselves would take in a special extraordinary session following the 38th General Session.

Many legislators were convinced that they would not be re-elected. Lawmakers became more focused on the dire state of affairs of state government.

As a result, political rancor was minimized and bipartisanship flourished, especially among the younger members of the Legislature.

Regardless of the position they might take, they were suddenly all dedicated to doing that which they believed was necessary to prepare Idaho for the challenges of the twentieth century

Never again will so many issues be tackled in one session in today's politically myopic, partisan times.

It is hard to believe that there will ever be another such perfect political storm of opportunity. A group of truly dedicated and extremely talented people was able to harness the energy of that unique opportunity to accomplish a vast range of significant, far-reaching legislative goals.

Public Demand For Services Outruns Willingness To Pay, Smylie Says

BOISE — Robert E. Smylie has been governor of Idaho 10 years today.

On this date in 1955 he told the opening joint session of the 33rd Legislature "our biggest task" was properly financing necessary state programs.

Recently he told a reporter the "greatest unsolved problem" facing Idaho is to devise "an adequate financial structure for the general fund."

He does believe the state is moving toward the "broader and more attractive revenue structure — one that produces more money" which he says Idaho needs. He believes that "the only excuse for a tax is to let people spend more money."

Willing To Speak Out

The governor is — and has been since he started his second term in 1959 and grew bold enough to criticize legislatures to their face — critical of "the Legislative willingness to overspend an executive budget" and the Legislature's and public's "desire for more services than the revenue structure will support."

He says "The hallmark of the 10 years has been an appetite for public expenditure that outran the will to pay. The people were searching for courage to meet their own aspirations. But this is characteristic of all our states."

On one phase of Idaho's revenue structure the governor has words of praise. Idaho's "greatest step forward" during the decade, he thinks, has been "a modern highway system which

we are well on the way to completing. The larger cities in eastern Idaho are now equidistant from Boise. There are better north - south communications. Construction is on or ahead of schedule. In my 1954 campaign I promised that the

ROBERT E. SMYLIE

Lewis-Clark Highway would be finished before I left office. It took two terms, but it is completed.

"1955 marks the point of stabilization in our highway revenue structure. We abandoned the $5 license plate. We may have to re-examine our license plate costs some day, but that day is not yet here."

The governor believes the fed-

eral government made a wise and proper move in undertaking the interstate highway system, largely at federal expense. But he gives state governments credit for it, too, saying it "developed in 1956 from joint meetings of governors and federal officials."

In the general field of federal-state relationships, Governor Smylie, who has served on the White House Committee on Intergovernmental Affairs since 1958, believes the states are making progress and getting more leeway in the parts they play in carrying out welfare and other federal programs.

Perhaps Necessary

"Centralization is bad per se if it is not necessary," he says. And that feeling is also what led him to work for the organization and strengthening of the Republican Governors Ass'n. The progress of that association in its first two years has been a source of deep personal satisfaction to him.

"The gutters full of water when the storm sewers are plugged prove that people are interested in policies other than national policies," he notes. "The association allows us to take a national look at local issues.

"Some of the best merchandise we've got is in the department labeled 'States of the Union.' Some of the best Republican records are in terms of social welfare at the state level while the Democrats are running to Washington.

"The national minority must

traditionally take a negative role, or thinks it must. Local winners can be positive. We have 17 Republican governors and they govern almost a majority of the nation's population.

"Strong states in a strong union are what will make federalism work. Neither can be weak at the expense of the other without depriving the people of the benefits of the system."

Smylie's greatest disappointment during his 10 years in office, he says, has been "the inability to rally opinion for constitutional reform and revision, which will be necessary before the state can achieve its full potential."

Here, the governor leaves himself open to the frequently-repeated criticism that he has not provided leadership and that the "inability to rally" is his own fault. One Republican leader, asked what he considers the most significant aspects of Smylie's administration, replied:

"He has been a fine administrative governor and he has given this state a lot of much-needed publicity, but he has exerted no leadership at all. And that's too bad, because he could have been a real hero."

Gets A Chuckle

This "lack of leadership" charge is one that has been debated for years and likely will be debated for at least two more years. The governor, himself, has been known to chuckle over a Lewiston Morning Tribune editorial of two years ago which said referring to Smylie: "Leadership, says the man who so often has been blamed for lack of it by those who refused to

Tax reform in Idaho

For years, tax reform in the State of Idaho had been bedeviled by what occurred after the action of the 23rd Legislature, when an extraordinary session in March of 1935 passed the Cooperative Emergency Revenue Act, commonly known as the Idaho Sales Tax Law.

C. Ben Ross

Governor C. Ben Ross, Democrat, had called the special session after the regular session of the 23rd Legislature had failed to raise revenue to provide the money required to meet the matching funds for the United States Emergency Relief of Unemployment. The federal government had already advanced $8 million to Idaho in an effort to try to relieve the severe recession that prevailed in the United States. The special legislative session passed a one-cent sales tax to provide the required matching funds.

A referendum was filed, and in November 1936 voters repealed the sales tax. Governor Ross was nailed with the "a Penny for Benny" tag that defeated him and many of those legislators who had voted for the tax measure.

From that Election Day forward it became an article of faith in Idaho politics that to touch the sales tax was to commit political suicide.

In 1955, businessman, farmer, and Canyon County Representative George Crookham had persuaded himself that the sales tax was the only way to raise the revenue required to provide a modicum of growth and stability in Idaho. Crookham had analyzed the issue and had found that the federal government had effectively foreclosed states from any additional income-tax revenue from either individuals or corporations; he also found that the property tax on residences in Idaho had reached a level that was overly burdensome to the average wage earner and had a negative impact on commercial expansion.

Crookham concluded that the sales tax was the appropriate method to alleviate the revenue woes of the state. As a member of the House Revenue and Taxation Committee, Crookham drafted sales tax bills in each session and mailed a copy of his proposed legislation to the key businesses that were the principal employers and significant taxpayers within the state. Sears, Roebuck and Company, JC Penney, Idaho Power, and others were targets. Crookham invited these institutions to advise him of the impact of a sales tax on them and their reaction to it. He analyzed the responses he received each year and then attempted to modify legislation to meet objections.

In 1961, as chairman of the House Revenue and Taxation Committee, Crookham was finally able to have a bill reported out of the committee to the House, where it was promptly defeated. Crookham then decided to run for governor on a sales tax ticket. The 1962 primary election handed him a deadly blow by the paucity of votes he received. Crookham retired from the political arena and directed his full efforts to the growth of his seed business in Caldwell.

By 1962 several other individuals, some of them younger and more willing to venture into the fray, also concluded that a sales tax was the only answer to Idaho's growing problems. Idaho faced a stagnant economy, a public education system woefully underfunded, and a tax structure that discouraged rather than encouraged growth. The real property tax and income tax on both individuals and corporations were clearly smothering growth.

These individuals analyzing the referendum vote of 1936, by which the initial Idaho sales tax venture failed, showed that the defeat was not as dramatic as had become an accepted myth. The 1936 votes by county were:

	County	Total Vote	In Favor	Against	Percent
1.	Ada	16,152	6,344	9,808	39.3
2.	Adams	932	492	440	52.8
3.	Bannock	10,865	5,018	5,847	46.2
4.	Bear Lake	2,404	1,266	1,138	52.7
5.	Benewah	2,389	1,242	1,147	52
6.	Bingham	5,009	2,289	2,720	45.7
7.	Blaine	1,393	687	706	49.3
8.	Boise	1,073	477	596	44.5
9.	Bonner	4,530	2,433	2,097	53.7
10.	Bonneville	5,911	2,513	3,398	42.5
11.	Boundary	1,386	671	715	48.4
12.	Butte·	704	383	321	54.4
13.	Camas	598	198	400	33.1
14.	Canyon	11,004	4,382	6,622	39.8
15.	Caribou	650	334	316	51.4
16.	Cassia	3,381	1,881	1,500	55.6
17.	Clark	468	170	298	36.3
18.	Clearwater	2,090	1,154	936	55.2
19.	Custer	933	550	383	58.9
20.	Elmore	2,186	1,009	1,177	46.2
21.	Franklin	2,634	1,209	1,425	45.9
22.	Fremont	2,699	1,488	1,211	55.1
23.	Gem	2,746	1,486	1,260	54.1
24.	Gooding	3,063	1,261	1,802	41.2
25.	Idaho	3,365	1,565	1,800	46.5
26.	Jefferson	2,648	1,387	1,261	52.4
27.	Jerome	2,685	1,200	1,485	44.7
28.	Kootenai	6,140	3,374	2,766	55
29.	Latah	3,583	1,982	1,601	55.3

30.	Lemhi	1,958	1,139	819	58.2
31.	Lewis	1,639	970	669	59.2
32.	Lincoln	1,190	472	718	39.7
33.	Madison	2,276	1,326	950	58.3
34.	Minidoka	2,222	1,204	1,018	54.2
35.	Nez Perce	5,264	3,281	1,983	62.3
36.	Oneida	1,591	889	702	55.9
37.	Owyhee	1,483	684	799	46.1
38.	Payette	3,116	1,082	2,034	34.7
39.	Power	1,285	605	680	47..1
40.	Shoshone	5,187	2,432	2,755	46.9
41:	Teton	892	548	344	61.6
42.	Twin Falls	8,256	3,836	4,420	46.5.
43.	Valley	1,774	659	1,115	37.1
44.	Washington	2,442	1,156	1,286	47.3

Despite an extreme depression, there had been only a narrow margin of defeat in most counties.

The new pro-sales tax coalition consisted of virtually all of the Ada, Bannock, and Twin Falls County delegations and a considerable number of Canyon County representatives, who were all willing to touch that third rail of Idaho politics, the sales tax. Most of them had run for office on a pro-sales tax stand, stressing that a sizable portion of the tax would go to tax reform and then to education, which was in critical need of realistic funding. A cautious politician, Governor Smylie, in his 1963 State of the State message, indicated that if the legislature was willing to pass a sales tax bill, he could under certain conditions approve it. That gave the issue the momentum of legitimacy and major public awareness. However, Smylie did not include any tax reform revenue or propose the tax in the budget he submitted to the 37th Legislature.

On the morning the sales tax was to be voted on in the House, an unexpected negative sales tax editorial was published in the *Idaho Daily Statesman*. Despite that, the House passed the first sales and use tax bill of the 1960s, combined with significant tax reform. It lowered the income-tax rate for individuals and corporations and lowered the real property tax by eliminating most of the taxing elements that were generating state revenue. The bill was then sent to the Senate for its consideration.

In the Senate, as in the House, the opposition came primarily from those counties bordering Oregon, Washington, Nevada, Utah, and Wyoming. Those counties bordering Washington felt they would lose the existing advantage they had of not having a sales tax while the state of Washington did. Those bordering Oregon were certain that Ontario would become a metropolis because Idaho business and customers would flee to a non-sales tax environment. Counties in southeastern Idaho bordering Utah did not want to lose the advantage they had and feared that Salt Lake City would become even more dominant than it was presently. Another group of senators were certain that the passage of the sales tax would open the floodgates to far greater state expenditures, which they opposed.

After extensive delay and maneuvering, the Senate defeated the sales tax bill.

Following this Senate action, the members of the Senate and of the House spent most of the remaining session polarized by the Senate's refusal to pass tax reform.

The battle waged over the sales tax and tax reform in the 37th Session resulted in wide publicity of the issues. In the 1964 legislative campaign, candidates maximized them. When the oratory ended, all members of the 37th Session who had supported the sales tax were reelected. Their arguments had persuaded Idaho voters that the sales tax and general tax reform were necessary to put the state on the right track for a sound, prosperous future.

Now, a majority of the 38th Session of the Idaho Legislature must be persuaded that the people were right.

Supporters of Sales Tax Hold Retail Store Edge

The 24 senators in the Idaho Legislature who were successful Tuesday in turning down a proposed three per cent sales and use tax represent counties which in 1962 accounted for about only 33 per cent of total dollars spent in retail sales.

On the other hand, the 20 senators who sought to pass the measure, which Gov. Robert E. Smylie says is necessary for the state to move ahead, represent counties where in the same year the dollars spent in retail sales amounted to about 67 per cent of the total.

Retail sales in Idaho in 1962 totaled just under $1 billion—$904,514,000 to be exact. Of this total, the 20 senators voting for the measure represent counties where $621,755,000 was spent in retail sales.

On the other hand, the 24 senators who downed the sales tax bill represent counties where retail sales totaled $282,-759,000.

The percentage of those who favor the sales tax would have been even greater had not one senator, whose county had retail sales of $2,588,000, switched his affirmative vote to no so he would be able to be on the prevailing side and able to vote for reconsideration of the outcome.

Also, statistics show the percentage in favor of the sales tax likely would have been even greater when note is taken that Idaho's retail sales have shown an increase of 16 per cent between 1958 and 1963.

The senators who voted for and against the sales tax, their counties and retail sales for 1962 follow:

FOR		AGAINST	
Barron, Camas ..$	676,000	Harn, Clark ......$	866,000
Beal, Butte	4,072,000	McClure, Payette .	13,363,000
Brooks, Blaine ..	7,297,000	Meadows, Power .	5,736,000
Dunn, Bear Lake	10,430,000	Murphy, Lincoln .	2,588,000
Ellsworth, Lemhi	7,932,000	Nally, Gem	11,117,000
Forsgren,		Ryan, Wash.	13,368,000
Franklin	10,358,000	Samuelson,	
Hansen, Minidoka	16,603,000	Bonner	19,792,000
Howe, Boundary .	8,260,000	Seeley, Jerome ...	12,401,000
Loveland, Cassia	25,401,000	Whitworth,	
Roden, Ada	144,791,000	Caribou	5,884,000
Schwendiman,		Yarbrough,	
Fremont	9,443,000	Owyhee	6,214,000
Swisher, Bannock	67,022,000	Ausich, Custer ...	2,910,000
Yensen, Boise ...	835,000	Bean, Valley	5,575,000
Young, Canyon ..	78,550,000	Chase, Benewah .	6,562,000
Andrus,		Collett, Elmore ..	13,244,000
Clearwater	8,769,000	Crawford, Lewis .	4,362,000
Lough, Latah	26,084,000	Daniels, Oneida ..	3,985,000
Rigby, Madison .	12,942,000	Dee, Idaho	14,042,000
Sandberg,		Egbert, Teton	2,635,000
Bingham	29,138,000	Frederickson,	
Wood, Bonneville	79,877,000	Gooding	10,300,000
Blick, Twin Falls	74,027,000	Glenn, Adams	2,512,000
		Moore, Nez Perce	53,274,000
		Murphy, Shoshone	25,041,000
		Tibbitts,	
		Jefferson	10,893,000
		Webster, Kootenai	36,101,000
Totals $621,755,000		Totals $282,759,000	

Smylie Asks Sales Tax To Finance Education; Apportioning Delayed

Talk Slaps At Racing, Primary

By JOHN CORLETT
Statesman Political Editor

Gov. Robert E. Smylie Tuesday asked the legislature to help put Idaho on the move toward a "new day of opportunity and new day of achievement" by enacting a sales tax to finance greater efforts in education, health, welfare and conservation.

It was the governor's sixth "State of the State" message to an Idaho Legislature, and it was the first time he flatly called for enactment of a sales tax.

Declaring that "penny pinching will have no political virtue," the governor strongly emphasized that in this 36th session "education is the prime issue," and called for greater spending in that field.

He told reporters he would detail in his budget message, to be delivered sometime next week, the kind of sales tax he thought the legislature should enact and the size of a budget needed to "catch up" with the long expanding needs of education and other services. The governor told the legislature that "in the field of governmental finance, this session will find its greatest challenge."

Message Gets Ovation

When the governor concluded his 4,000 word speech — one of the shortest — he was accorded the longest standing ovation ever given him in the legislature.

Both Democrats and Republicans praised his message, and two legislators said the governor

"If there had been willingness to spend more ... in the decade before this one," said the governor, "we would not be so far behind now ... I am convinced to the strongest educational system we can possibly afford."

The House chamber where the governor talked to the joint session was quiet when he said:

"The budget when it reaches you will be based upon, and will recommend, the enactment of a retail sale and use tax designed to produce revenue adequate to the needs of these expanded services."

Tax Reform Added

"I AM COMMITTED to the strongest possible educational system we can possibly afford," Gov. Robert E. Smylie told the Idaho legislature on Tuesday. To pay the cost for improved education, he proposed a sales tax.

Measure Proposed By Districts

Gem Senate Passes Bill For Seaport

The Idaho Senate approved Monday a bill implementing a constitutional amendment authorizing port districts to issue revenue bonds.

Idaho has only one port district, at Lewiston.

LEWISTON MORNING TRIBUNE

Established September, 1892   (AP)—Associated Press   LEWISTON, IDAHO — CLARKSTON, WASH., WEDNESDAY, JANUARY 6, 1965   14 Pages   Single Copies 10 Cents

Smylie Proposes Sales Tax To Finance Progress

SMYLIE ADDRESSES LEGISLATURE — Gov. Robert E. Smylie was shown at the rostrum yesterday in the House of Representatives chamber at Boise as he delivered his "State of the State" message to the Idaho Legislature. The Spotlight was Smylie's endorsement of a sales tax to finance a big increase in state spending. (AP Wirephoto)

Program Praised, Slapped

Solons Propose Submitting Sales Tax To Voters

BOISE (AP) — A sales tax subject to confirmation by voters was suggested Tuesday as a way to solve Idaho's knotty financial problem.

It was coupled with a proposal that—if a sales tax is enacted and property and income tax rates reduced —the latter could not be increased without approval of the people.

Head Tax Boost Is Urged By Foes Of Sales Tax

BOISE (AP) — Opponents of the sales tax voiced renewed objections to such a levy in the Idaho Legislature Wednesday, offering an increase in the head tax as an alternative.

The Joint Finance-Appropriations Committee failed again to come up with a total general fund budget, but continued at work in an effort to reach agreement.

Long Lines Up With South On Filibustering

A new tax reform strategy

Del Lowe

Phil Peterson

Following the defeat of the tax reform package in the 37th Legislature, an ad-hoc committee that had in that session conducted research, drafted legislation, and led sales tax efforts, consisting of Del Lowe, a leading CPA; Phillip Peterson, a University of Idaho Law School professor; and practicing attorney Chuck McDevitt, Ada County legislator, reviewed the principal objections to the sales tax and companion bills that constituted the tax reform measures introduced in the 37th Session.

The chief complaint was that too much tax relief had been given to corporations because of the property-tax reductions combined with the income tax reductions.

Adjustments were made by the ad-hoc committee to attempt to deal with the objections. Their goal was to have something ready to present to the House Revenue and Tax Committee at the beginning of the 38th Session.

Lowe continued to refine his economic data so that he could project with some accuracy the revenue that would be generated by a sales and use tax, which in turn would give the legislative committee the ability to deal more comfortably with the amount of real property and income tax relief that might be granted in the companion measures.

Peterson and McDevitt addressed the issues that had been raised by lawyers examining the legislation that had been proposed and then strengthened the language and finalized the legislation for introduction in the 38th Session.

John Dahl, J.R. Simplot

Early in the 37th Session J.R. (Jack Simplot), a prominent Idaho businessman, had asked this ad hoc committee to meet with him and his financial officer, John Dahl. Simplot wanted to have a thorough understanding of the tax reform legislation that was being proposed in that Session.

Likewise, in the 38th Session, Simplot requested another meeting to review changes made and the updated economic data forecast by Lowe. These meetings would later prove to be invaluable in the passage of the Idaho Sales Tax Reform Law and the subsequent referendum on the tax measure.

Sales Tax Bill Drafted 'With Care And Caution'

BOISE (AP) — The chairman of the House Revenue and Taxation Committee said Saturday that when a sales tax bill is introduced in the Idaho Legislature it will have had more consideration "than any similar bill ever introduced."

Rep. Arvil Millar, R-Bingham, said his tax writing committee is moving with "care and caution" in drafting a sales tax bill, and predicted it would be ready for introduction sometime next week.

Millar said he plans to have the bill acted on in the House by the second week of February.

Meanwhile, Senate President Pro Tem Jack Murphy, R-Lincoln, said he is working to assure that if a sales tax is enacted, a special referendum election will be held so the voters can approve or reject it.

He said it appears the legislature cannot by statute propose its own special referendum, and that he now is giving consideration to proposing changes in the law, including a provision for a special election in May.

YOUR PHYSI

3-Per-Cent Sales Tax Bill Introduced In Idaho House

BOISE (AP) — A 3 per cent sales and use tax to finance a $135 million general fund budget for the 1965-67 fiscal period was introduced Friday in the House of Representatives.

The proposed levy would raise an estimated $56 million each biennium and would permit at least $26 million in income and property tax relief.

The sales tax bill was introduced by the House Revenue & Taxation Committee which also sent to the House floor a

★　　★　　★　　　　★　　★　　★

Farm Bureau income tax proposal calling for a 2½ per cent levy on adjusted gross income before deductions.

The bureau presented the proposal as an alternative to a sales tax and contends it would bring in an additional $10 mil-

★　　★　　★

lion in revenue per biennium.

That levy would be in addition to the tax now levied on income. A companion measure would repeal the 8-mill c o u n t y levy for the state school foundation program as long as the 2½ per cent income surtax was in effect.

A third bill would provide for

Moving forward in the 38th

Arvil Millar - Bingham

After the organization of the 38th Idaho Legislature, the Revenue and Taxation Committee met, reelected Arvil Millar (Bingham) chairman, and chose Chuck McDevitt (Ada) as vice chairman.

Most of the members of that committee in the 37th Session continued to serve on the committee in the 38th, so the members were familiar with what had been proposed two years earlier and now addressed the issues that had been raised then in the new package of legislation.

As is true with any tax measure, the impact on various elements of the state and various segments of the economy differ. In order to meet the concerns of members of the committee, changes were made in the proposed legislation; but none were of great substance nor changed the character of the tax reform package that would be presented in the five bills.

Tremendous pressure was brought on the Revenue and Taxation Committee and the ad-hoc committee by numerous groups and individuals seeking an exemption from the application of the sales and use tax, but the committee held firm on limiting exemptions. The "Sales and Use Tax Exemption Section" lists Exemption A though Q (not including subparts). Most would fall under the category of "Production

Exemption," which categorizes those items that are purchased to be included in or sold as part of an item or items grown or produced for resale.

In years since the adoption of the sales and use tax, it appears that by and large, the legislature has never met an "exemption" that it did not like. As a result, as of this time, there are presently 46 exemptions to the Idaho Sales and Use Tax with an estimated fiscal value of more than $1 billion.

Charles F. McDevitt-Ada

In the 37th Session, Arvil Millar had not felt sufficiently comfortable with the many details of the sales and use tax bill and so had designated Charles McDevitt to carry it.

Millar was offended by the strong attacks on McDevitt in his debate of the bill, so in the 38th Session he concluded that he would carry the sales tax bill himself, with McDevitt handling the details of the complex related package of legislation.

James W. Monroe -Nez Perce

In the 38th Session as in the 37th, the opposition to the legislation was led by Jimmy Monroe (Nez Perce). Monroe, a Democrat, was knowledgeable about almost all elements of Idaho's tax structure, as he had chaired the Revenue and Taxation Committee in 1959, the last session in which Democrats had controlled the House of Representatives. Monroe's opposition to a sales and use tax was based primarily on the fear that he shared with many of the business people in Nez Perce and surrounding counties: if Idaho adopted a sales tax, it would lose the advantage it currently had over businesses in the state of Washington, and Lewiston's neighbor just across the Snake River, Clarkston, would grow and prosper to the disadvantage of Lewiston, Nez Perce County, and the surrounding business area.

Evidence of this pressure from constituents on legislators from border counties was contained in testimony before the Rev and Tax Committee.

Two prominent Payette County businessmen, Leo Marsters and Toby Massengill, representing residents and businesses of Payette, Weiser, and New Plymouth, testified. Marsters stated that if a sales tax was passed "less of revenue and businesses in border communities would result in less income for the State."

They further argued that collection of the tax would fall on a small number of retailers, making it an unfair discrimination against Idaho shop owners, and that businessmen would "flow to Ontario, Oregon."

An open letter to the legislature opposing the sales tax, signed by twenty-one Weiser and Payette residents and published in local and statewide newspapers, stated: "Such a tax is unjust to low income families; is unjust to retired people with fixed incomes, and is unfair to border communities."

The border counties' opposition was summed up in the closing remarks in debate by Monroe: "If a sales tax is enacted the principal beneficiary will be Clarkston, Washington."

Monroe was a clever opponent, but the needs of the State of Idaho were so great that the tide of tax reform was sweeping away lesser concerns.

The sales and use tax and accompanying bills comprising the tax reform package passed the House on February 24, 1965, by a vote of 49 to 30.

The House bill and accompanying legislation was then transmitted to the Senate, where the opposition was far more dedicated and certainly more entrenched.

LEWISTON MORNING TRIBUNE

Established September, 1892   (AP)—Associated Press   LEWISTON, IDAHO ~ CLARKSTON, WASH., THURSDAY, FEBRUARY 25, 1965   Two Sections ~ 32 Pages   Single Copies 10 Cents

Idaho House Approves 3 Per Cent Sales Tax

Three Per Cent Sales Tax Passes House by 19 Votes With Other Levies Reduced

Jam-Packed Galleries Listen to Sales Tax Debate

PERRY SWISHER
BANNOCK

On Tuesday, March 22, 1965, the bill came up for consideration by the Senate. In an unusual move, the Senate approved the presence of the vice chair of the House Revenue and Taxation Committee on the Senate floor to assist the senator carrying the bill.

Perry Swisher (Bannock) carried the measure in the Senate; he was brilliant in his command of details and was a highly persuasive orator. At the beginning of the debate, the gallery was full; there was standing room only.

MARY T. BROOKS
BLAINE

The debate went on, ranging from eloquent to mundane, causing Senator Mary Brooks (Blaine), late in the day, to rise on a point of personal privilege at the end of three and a half hours of debate.

She stated, "I rise simply to point out that women do not do all of the talking."

She then sat back in her seat, having made her point.

The gallery began to thin out at an increasing rate as the debate raged on for another hour and a half, at which point it was virtually empty. There is no evidence that the ending of the debate was caused by the absence of the gallery population, but it was an interesting coincidence. The vote was 20-24. When the measure failed, senators moved to reconsider the bill, thereby keeping the measure alive.

At that time, the key question for leadership was what to do with the bill.

GEORGE L. BLICK
TWIN FALLS - MAJORITY LEADER

It was on the third-reading calendar of the Senate and had to be referred to a committee pending its being scheduled for another vote. The situation was complicated by the fact that no major Senate committee chair did not opposed passage of the sales tax. The Senate left the problem unresolved and adjourned for the day.

After a day's contemplation and party caucuses, the Bill was referred to the Gubernatorial Appointments Committee, a seldom heard-of and rarely used committee.

It would withhold the bill from being sent forward for action one more time; its chairman was Senator Blick (Twin Falls), the Senate Majority Leader, a tax advocate.

The senators voting against the bill represented just 35 percent of the Idaho population, while those representing 65 percent supported it.

The Senate vote was as follows:

For	census	Against	census
Barron, Camas	917	Harn, Clark	915
Beal, Butte	3,498	McClure, Payette	12,363
Brooks, Blaine	4,598	Meadows, Power	4,111
Dunn, Bear Lake	7,148	Murphy, Lincoln	3,686
Ellsworth, Lemhi	5,816	Nally, Gem	9,127
Forsgren, Franklin	8,457	Ryan, Washington	8,378
Hansen, Minidoka	14,394	Samuelson, Bonner	15,587
Howe, Boundary	5,809	Seeley, Jerome	11,712
Loveland, Cassia	16,121	Whitworth, Caribou	5,976
Roden, Ada	93,460	Yarbrough, Owyhee	6,375
Schwendiman, Frem't	8,679	Aussich, Custer	2,996
Swisher, Bannock	49,342	Bean, Valley	3,663
Yensen, Boise	1,646	Chase, Benewah	6,036
Young, Canyon	57,662	Collett, Elmore	16,719
Andrus, Clearwater	8,548	Crawford, Lewis	4,423
Lough, Latah	21,170	Daniels, Oneida	3,603
Rigby, Madison	9,417	Dee, Idaho	13,542
Sandberg, Bingham	28,218	Egbert, Teton	2,639
Wood, Bonneville	46,906	Frederickson, Gooding	9,544
Blick, Twin Falls	41,842	Glenn, Adams	2,978
		Moore, Nez Perce	27,066
		Murphy, Shoshone	20,876
		Tibbitts, Jefferson	11,672
		Webster, Kootenai	29,556
Total:	**433,648**	**Total:**	**233,543**

Flaus New Day

ARTHUR WILSON, right, secretary of the Senate, presents to Lt. Gov. W. E. Drevlow the Senate roll call which passed the measure imposing a three per cent sales tax, scheduled to be collected beginning July 1. The vote was 26 to 18.

public schools. The amend-   Six Change Votes   Roden Sees Necessity

The Senate quickly made it clear to the House and to the public that there were the votes necessary to pass the sales tax in the Senate provided the House acted on two specific issues:

1. A bill dictating that a special referendum election allow the Idaho citizenry to have the final say on the sales tax before the tax could become effective on July 1.

2. A new school equalization formula that would create a new system of the distribution of state school funds.

On the day the Senate initially defeated the sales tax bill, the House of Representatives still had before it the school appropriation measure that had been amended by the Senate to create additional funding for school districts with between 400 and 700 students.

A separate bill in the Senate Education Committee would appropriate an additional $1 million to fund remote schools that, under the educational funding bill and formula, would now receive at least $10.00 per average student daily attendance, the average being provided under the proposed new formula. The Senate sought assurances that that measure would be favorably dealt with in the House.

An unusual joint caucus between the Republicans in the Senate and in the House was proposed and held to clear the processes under which the separate bodies might proceed to satisfy the demands of each other. The Senate Democratic caucus had also gotten the vice chair of the House Revenue and Tax Committee to appear before it to answer detailed sales tax questions.

The school apportionment bill, one of those key bills that the Senate sought action on, was progressing rapidly on the House calendar so that it could be considered at virtually any time.

Minority Leader Darrell Manning and Herman McDevitt (Bannock) were fearful that if that bill passed, the House's only leverage with the Senate would be lost, so McDevitt initiated a slowdown in the House by simply demanding, as the rules allowed, that each bill or measure be read aloud word for word by the House Clerk. Needless to say, this brought the House to a virtual standstill.

H.J. McDevitt - Bannock

Don Pieper-Bonneville

Speaker Cenarrusa calmly conducted the affairs of the House by adjourning late on the first day of the slowdown and setting shorter sessions after that first day so legislators were not exhausted by the long hours.

When Herman McDevitt needed for personal reasons to leave the floor, other Members of the House, notably Don Pieper (Bonneville), would enforce the rules of the House by refusing to waive them. A single objection defeats that motion.

The school appropriation bill had been amended by the House to appropriate funds for the remote school districts, which the Senate had entertained in a separate bill. Manning and Herman McDevitt intended to continue the delay of progress on that bill being sought by the Senate.

Herman McDevitt's stated strategy had been to hold the final school appropriation bill and the funding formula measure hostage until the Senate acted on the sales tax: "I do not want the vote on this measure [the school formula bill] no matter how it goes to influence a vote in the Senate on the Sales Tax measures before the Senate."

From March 2 to March 11, daily negotiations took place between key House and Senate members.

Then on Thursday, March 11, HB 222 was put to the vote of the Senate. The vote was 26-18. The bill had finally passed.

Gov. Smylie Applauds Legislature

Gov. Robert E. Smylie Thursday night described the 38th Idaho Legislature as "one of the greatest, if not the greatest session in Idaho's history."

He made his statement on sine die adjournment of the legislature.

"Any one of a half-dozen pieces of legislation enacted in this session would prove a landmark of accomplishment standing alone," the governor said. "The budget makes adequate provision for providing effective solutions to many of the human problems of our people. The session acted with courage, talent and skill in moving to do what must be done, and in being willing to face the music and pay the bills."

WILLIAM C. RODEN
ADA

The five accompanying measures dealing with real property and income tax reform and allocation of certain tax funds were considered in order and passed by the Senate; those measures were carried and expertly defended by Senator William "Bill" Roden (Ada).

Now the fate of the 1965 sales tax and tax reforms and the future direction of the Gem State would be decided by Idaho voters in the November 1966 election in a tax reform referendum.

Selling the sales tax

When the special session on reapportionment ended, the pro-sales tax reform forces kicked their campaign into high gear. They focused on persuading voters that their approval of the tax reform referendum would place Idaho on the right track to a sound fiscal future.

There have been references in some publications to one or two lonely individuals supporting the tax referendum. This simply was not the case. It took a cast of many to accomplish the final goal, but there were some who did contribute special effort. Legislators who sought reelection were quick to articulate their support for the tax reform legislation and its attendant significant increase of funding for public schools, both K-12 and higher education, as well as reductions in income and property taxes.

P.K. Harwood-Jefferson

Jack Simplot quietly informed his company's general counsel, Lloyd Haight, that he wanted to do everything possible to support the tax reform. Acting upon his employer's instructions, Haight contacted P.K. (Pat) Harwood, who had served in the 1965 Legislature as a representative from Jefferson County.

Haight's selection of Harwood proved to be a wise one. Harwood built an organization and personally traveled the length and breadth of the state, tirelessly speaking to local business groups, fraternities, and social organizations as well as editors of local papers and anyone else who would listen to him. He organized letter-writing campaigns, created a phone bank, and carried on one of the most effective election campaigns the state had ever seen.

The opposition to the sales tax and those seeking to have a majority vote to defeat the referendum were also very busy. The "Forward Idaho Committee" worked as hard to defeat the referendum as they had to defeat the legislation in the House and Senate; opponents were using the same arguments to convince people.

On the positive side, legislators appeared with local organizations using the materials provided by Harwood as well as the Electors Informative Plan pamphlet.

V. Ravenscroft-Gooding

Charles McDevitt publicly debated Vern Ravenscroft, a Democratic representative from Gooding County, in Twin Falls. Through the efforts of Harwood and funding by Simplot, individual legislators and elected officials provided positive information to the voters of Idaho.

In the end, the voters recognized that a sound fiscal Idaho future depended on their final approval, and they responded with a strong favorable vote.

Is This A Job For The Voters?

If the Idaho Legislature decides, after all its firm and fearless conversation, that it can't pass a tax bill without referring it to the voters for approval, the next item of legislative controversy presumably would be the wording of the referendum measure.

Obviously, the voters should have the same choices the legislators have if they are asked to take over the legislators' responsibilities. Therefore, it would seem impractical to refer to the voters for approval only one tax proposal.

Our own idea for a questionnaire to be submitted to the voters on some future ballot would be roughly as follows:

1. Do you favor increased state expenditures for education, health, welfare and other state services long neglected because appropriations were inadequate? (The voters' likely decision: an overwhelming "yes.")

2. Would you favor a sales tax to raise the money? (Likely answer: a resounding "no.")

3. Would you favor sharp increases in income taxes to raise the money? (Likely reply: absolutely no!)

After careful consideration of the election results, the 1967 or 1969 Legislature presumably would have all the facts it needs to make a firm and fearless decision — to wit: all the facts the legislators also have right now.

State Sen. Jack Murphy, R-Lincoln, Senate majority leader, tossed the referendum idea into the legislative mill the other day. His idea was that the Legislature should pass a sales tax this year, then submit the law to the voters for approval in a special election.

Naturally, nobody was anxious to oppose this idea too pointedly in the Legislature. Any legislator speaking out against it might arouse the wrath of many voters who would accuse him of trying to deprive the citizens of the right to judge their own affairs.

On the other hand, many legislators must have winced privately. If they approve a sales tax (or a higher income tax) to finance the state programs they obviously must approve in this session, what would happen to those programs in the coming bienium if the new tax was repudiated at the polls? Teachers who had received salary raises presumably would have them revoked. Universities and colleges that had started long-delayed programs of major importance would have to abandon them. In every branch of state government, agencies which have been skimping along for years would step at last upon solid footing — then suddenly find they were sunk in quicksand.

Gov. Robert E. Smylie was among those who skirted rather cautiously around the Murphy land mine. He said the referendum might be a good idea, but the state could save $500,000 by submitting the question to voters in the 1966 general election, rather than in a special election this year. If a referendum is necessary at all, this proposal would have certain advantages. It would give voters almost two years of experience with higher taxes to get accustomed to paying them — and observing the benefits of adequate state appropriations. It would give the state almost two years of sound government before the voters decided whether to wreck it by cutting off its needed revenues. And, incidentally, it would enable Smylie to complete his current term without the necessity of presiding over utter chaos.

It might be argued that a tax referendum is likely whether the legislators institute it or not. If the Legislature imposes higher taxes, either by the sales or income tax route, somebody is likely to start circulating petitions to have the new tax killed by the voters in an election. Perhaps Murphy — and the many legislators he presumably represents as Senate majority leader — figure they might as well have the public credit, at least, for letting the voters decide.

However, if the voters must take over the legislators' hardest responsibility, they at least should have some choices on the ballot — not just one tax plan.

And many voters, we suspect, would prefer that the legislators do their own work, on the theory that this is what they were elected to do.

If they sincerely believe, after studying all the facts which the ordinary citizen does not have at his disposal, that any given tax bill is necessary to serve the state, why don't they just pass it?

The worst that could happen would be that some of them might be turned out of office by infuriated voters in the next election. What is so terrifying about this prospect? To paraphrase the old army line: What's the matter? Do they want to legislate forever? — B. J.

On November 8, 1966, Idaho voters approved the Idaho sales tax referendum by a vote of 156,109 (61.18%) to 99,048 (38.82%).

Tax reform was now in truth an Idaho reality.

The organizing and leadership abilities of Pat Harwood persisted after the 1966 election. His organization ultimately became IACI, The Idaho Association of Commerce & Industry. Under Harwood's skillful craftsmanship, IACI became one of the most effective lobbying organizations in the state. The heretofore unknown young fellow from the upper Snake River would remain a powerful political force in the State of Idaho for many productive years.

Reapportionment

As soon as the 38th Session was adjourned, the Clerk of the House read a proclamation from Governor Smylie calling a special session for the purpose of reapportionment of the state legislature

The math had been done by the 37th Session's legislative counsel, providing the members of the legislature in the special session with the data required for them to begin discussion.

The variables were the size of the legislature and the population of the state—that is, how many members of the House and how many members of the Senate should make up a reapportioned legislature. This membership figure determined the size of the legislative districts—that is, how many people had to be within each legislative district in order to meet the criteria as set forth by the Supreme Court.

After some debate and discussion, the House and Senate determined the size that they felt appropriate for each of those bodies. Following that determination, the question then was: how on the maps of the state of Idaho provided for that purpose could you divide up the state to provide districts equivalent to the number of members required by the legislative determination of the size of the two bodies.

Early on, the issue most hotly debated was by and between the counties immediately surrounding or contiguous to Ada County; with the exception of Canyon County, all of them were quite small in population. How might one of these counties or several of them come together to form a district, taking just enough of Ada County to meet the number criterion without taking so much that they would lose the characteristics that then existed within those counties?

It was interesting to watch the smaller counties attempt to aggregate with a piece of Ada County in order to meet the minimum criterion. Part of this discussion was what would happen to the incumbent legislators from those counties or from one of those counties if more than one was required to arrive at a district sufficient in size with its borrowed numbers from Ada County. Each of the individuals involved in these discussions had an idea of the percentage of the population of their county whose votes they had received and what the results might be by joining together with another county and with a portion of Ada County.

A great deal of the collegiality and good humor that had existed throughout the 38th Session disappeared as several individuals tried to determine how they could join in compliance with the United States Supreme Court's decision and still maintain a position for themselves in the legislature.

The redistricting of Ada County of course had to wait until it could be determined what pieces of Ada County might be taken in creating a district for adjoining counties. In reviewing the votes from the last several general elections, it was apparent that no matter how Ada County was districted, one or more of the districts could readily become a Democrat-majority district based upon the vote tallies from those elections. This of course would change the character of what had been an all-Republican county in the representation in the Legislature.

Watching the drama was an interesting insight into human nature and the reactions of everyone as to their political future.

Order throughout the process was maintained, however, and in a short time the 38th Session's membership had once again performed its assigned duties in a workmanlike fashion, redistricting the State of Idaho in a manner that would be found by the Idaho Supreme Court to be in compliance with the criteria set down by the United States Supreme Court. (The variance permitted by the United States Supreme Court was a deviation from absolute one man-one vote of plus or minus ten percent.)

The reapportionment challenge would now get strict scrutiny from the Idaho Supreme Court to determine whether the legislature's idea of one man-one vote passed judicial review.

Meanwhile, political pundits were already extolling the achievements of the 38th Session of the Idaho Legislature.

Accomplishments of the 38th

"Any one of the half-dozen pieces of legislation enacted in this session would prove a landmark accomplishment standing alone." "The budget makes adequate provision for providing effective solutions to many of the human problems of our people. The session acted with courage, talent and skill in moving to do what must be done, and in being willing to face the music and pay the bills.". ...Governor Robert Smylie. The 38th Session of the Idaho Legislature between January 4 and March 18 passed the following legislation:

- Established the Idaho Water Board and the Idaho Department of Water Resources, calling for a statewide water plan.

- Real property, personal property, and public-utility operating property: uniform method of assessing like properties for taxing purposes (Idaho Supreme Court declared unconstitutional).

- Established the Urban Renewal Agency, the State Personnel Commission, and Department Merit System.

- Adopted the Administrative Procedures Act to prescribe rules and regulations for departments of state government.

- Initiated a 3-percent retail sales tax.

- Authorized condominiums.

- Established the Public Employee Retirement System.

- Created the Parks Board and Parks Department. Created Idaho Outfitters and Guides Board.

- Adopted the Judicial Retirement Act.

- Adopted the Idaho Private Contractors Licensing Act.

- Established the Idaho Pea & Lentil Commission.

- Established the Idaho Commission on Alcoholism.

- Established position of Executive Director of Higher Education.

- As part of the passage of the 3-percent sales tax, increased distribution of state liquor sales revenue to counties, cities, villages and the Permanent Building Fund. Reduced corporate income taxes from 10.5 percent of taxable income to 6 percent of taxable income.

- Eliminated the employer's share of teachers' Social Security taxes so long as the sales tax act remains in force and effect.

- Eliminated from the property tax rolls of the counties the contribution to the teachers' retirement system so long as the sales tax remains in force and effect. Prohibited the levy of a state ad valorem tax in any period during which a sales tax is in force in the state.

- Provided for creation of Community Mental Health Centers.

- Provided for Idaho State University to offer four-year college courses in general engineering with emphasis in nuclear science.

- Enacted an interstate library compact.

- Provided for the calling of a constitutional convention. Prohibited deceptive trade practices.

- Provided for the licensing of dealers and salesman of motor vehicles.

- Provided for a comprehensive study of the court system of the state by the Legislative Council. (Recommendation of Council later adopted by the Legislature).

- Authorized comprehensive study and preparation of legislation to adopt a Uniform Commercial Code by the 39th Legislature.

- Made unlawful the importing of lumber products into Idaho from any foreign country.

- Provided for creation of hospital districts.

- Provided for Boards of County Commissioners to pass ordinances, rules, and regulations. Provided for driver-training programs for all residents of the state ages 14 through 18 whether or not they are enrolled in public, private, or parochial school.

- Provided for licensing of commercial driver-training schools.

- Provided for qualification of blind persons for employment under any merit system in effect or hereafter to be established where sight is not essential to the performance of duties.

- Gave Boise Junior College four-year status and allowed the renamed Boise College to provide courses at the junior and senior class levels and to grant baccalaureate degrees.

- Designated Massacre State Park and Historical Monument.

- In special session, undertook historic reapportionment of the Senate and House of Representatives in conformance with the Constitution of the United States.

Among the most significant

IDAHO WATER RESOURCES MANAGEMENT

With all of the complexities involved in creating the legislation to manage Idaho's water resources, all of the principal players were involved, there was little opposition to the proposed legislation, and it passed handily. As essential as water is to the economic welfare of a high percentage of the citizens of Idaho and the state itself, Idaho had never before had a State Water Board nor a state water plan. The 38th Session created an Idaho Water Board and charged it with creating a state water plan, also providing the funding for these activities. The first state water plan was created under this Water Board working with the State Department of Water Resources and interested parties. Herman McDevitt, who helped draft the water legislation, was later appointed by the Governor to the Idaho Water Board and was active in the administration of Idaho's Water Plan. To this date, water plans are created on a regular basis by the State Water Board, action that is of significant importance to the water users and to those interested in locating in Idaho and in knowing what water resources are or might be available to them.

CREATION OF IDAHO STATE PARKS SYSTEM

Thanks in large measure to the efforts of Governor Smylie, the Harriman family—through brothers Averell and Roland Harriman, who owned the multi-thousand-acre Railroad Ranch in eastern Idaho—was prepared to donate that land to the state of Idaho upon certain conditions. The land now Harriman State Park is a rare jewel even in the jewel-rich Idaho crown. The North Fork (Henry's Fork) of the Snake River runs through the property, and it is dotted with several lakes upon which trumpeter swans reside during most of the year.

One of the principal conditions of the Harriman family's donation was the creation and operation of a State Parks Board and Parks Department able to manage and administer this property. Roland Harriman came to Boise and met with members of the legislature, urging them to consider this property as one that would be long remembered as a generous gift of the Harriman family.

Although there was some opposition to the acceptance of the gift, a substantial majority of the legislature saw the benefits of accepting such a gift even though the long-term management would involve significant cost. The 38th Session created a State Parks Board and Parks Department, with the board empowered to manage the department and the parks owned by the state.

To this day, the State Parks Department is doing and has done a tremendous job in the administration of all the state parks, and a visit to the Harriman Ranch is one that every citizen of Idaho should experience.

STUDY OF THE IDAHO COURT SYSTEM

Idaho's court system had long been operating as it was created, while the volume and complexity of the matters reaching the court system had changed and multiplied. Several states had undertaken realignments of their court systems, creating an initial magistrate court for the handling of misdemeanors with specialty judges dealing with probate matters and then an interim court between that magistrate court level and the Idaho Supreme Court to which the Supreme Court might direct cases that were of less complexity or were not precedent setting.

The 38th Session felt it was long past time that an analysis and study be made of the state court system to see how it might be changed or expanded in order to provide the citizens of the state with the best possible judicial system.

Such a comprehensive study was undertaken, and in subsequent years the legislature acted upon the recommendations flowing from this study.

THE ADMINISTRATIVE PROCEDURES ACT

Between 1945 and 1965, the administrative agencies of the state had grown in both number and size, yet they had no clear direction as to the procedures under which they should conduct their activities. Likewise, those appearing before administrative bodies in Idaho or affected by rules, regulations, or orders from those bodies, had no clear guide as to how they could proceed before the administrative agencies or seek relief from the actions of administrative agencies.

The 38th Session adopted the Administrative Procedures Act, which clearly prescribes the rules and regulations that control the procedures of state agencies and enables citizens to clearly understand what those procedures are and how they can receive relief from adverse actions of state agencies.

This action, although relatively unheralded at the time, was one of the more significant actions of the 38th Session.

ESTABLISHING URBAN RENEWAL

In 1965, anyone walking the business-district streets of Boise, Pocatello, Idaho Falls, Lewiston, or Coeur d 'Alene would see many dark storefronts as well as numerous buildings showing obvious need of attention.

The restoration or renewal of these properties could not be accomplished under existing legislation and existing ordinances and regulation of the municipal authorities.

The urban renewal legislation provided for the creation of an agency by a municipality to address these shortcomings, to cut through some of the red tape, and to provide funds out of the real property tax revenues for the management of the district itself as well as the properties under its jurisdiction.

This legislation, which has been amended several times since its creation, was able to accomplish great advances in the municipalities in the state. In retrospect, the 38th Session was remiss in not requiring a mandated sun-setting of any such agency.

THE IDAHO PERSONNEL COMMISSION

Under the adopted legislation, the state personnel system would be run as a system that would protect an employee, provide a procedure for grievance, and provide for all employees appealing specific actions by an administrator. The merit system was needed to provide employees protection against arbitrary action; Finally, it created a structure to ensure that those who sought relief under the personnel system would receive due process. All of these matters were addressed in the State Personnel Commission and Department created by the 38th Legislature.

Bill To Let Boise College Grant Degrees Is Approved

BOISE (AP) — A bill clearing the way for creation of a degree granting upper division at Boise Junior College was approved by the Idaho House of Representatives Thursday and sent to the Senate.

The vote on the measure, introduced by the Ada County delegation, was 64-1. The one dissenting vote was cast by Rep. George Brocke, D-Latah.

BOISE JUNIOR COLLEGE

The Ada County delegation (which then acted as the representatives for the entire Ada County) acted to take steps that were in the best interests of Ada County in its entirety. The ability of the then Boise Junior College to grant baccalaureate degrees was critical for the growth of that institution. As usual, just having the name "Boise" attached to the legislation raised some difficulty statewide, and the Ada County delegation was unsure of their ability to pass this measure. The Lewiston Port Authority needed revenue bond authority as well as the right to lease property to third parties. The Ada County delegation agreed to support the required legislation of the Port Authority in exchange for Nez Perce and adjacent counties not actively opposing the measure permitting Boise Junior College to become a four-year institution and grant baccalaureate degrees. This and other political vote "trades" passed the necessary legislation; Boise Junior College was now a four-year institution renamed Boise College and able to grant baccalaureate degrees.

IDAHO STATE UNIVERSITY

Idaho State University had been interacting with the federal atomic-energy site near Arco and had begun to develop some interesting educational opportunities in connection with the work that it had pioneered with the site and with the Atomic Energy Commission in Idaho Falls. The Bannock County and other eastern Idaho delegations sought authority to create a Nuclear Science curriculum at Idaho State University, resulting in a Nuclear Science Degree. The delegations from eastern Idaho and the delegation from Ada County had agreed to support each other's educational institutions' requests. Idaho State embraced its Nuclear Engineering path.

PUBLIC SCHOOL EDUCATION

The 38th Session increased funds for higher education by 22 percent over the prior year's level; increased funding for public-school systems (K-12) by more than 42 percent; created two new positions on the Board of Education; and created the position of Executive Director of Higher Education, who was granted ex officio membership in the State Board of Education, all with the view of invigorating Idaho's education opportunities.

Because of a new formula passed by the 38th Session, the distribution of an additional $61 million in state aid to public schools resulted. The distribution formula for public education and supplemental appropriation of $2 million to rural schools were critical to the passage of the tax reform bills. The jockeying over their passage and the timing of their passage between the House and the Senate were the principal factors in the 38th Legislature remaining in session past a sixty-day limitation.

Ironically, many of those ardent opponents of the Tax Reform Act represented small or remote school districts who were the major beneficiaries of the $2 million-dollar increment of the Educational Distribution Formula, which was made possible by the passage of the 3-percent sales tax and accompanying legislation.

Solon Says Bill Would Add $1 Million In Tax Revenue

* * * * * *

'Famous Potatoes' Slogan Survives

BOISE (AP)—The Idaho Senate refused Friday to eliminate the "Famous Potatoes" slogan from the state's automobile license plates after it was told that the words "Idaho" and "potatoes" are synonymous.

The vote was 12-32, which Sen. Vincent Nally, R-Gem, advised the Senate was the exact vote by which the sales tax bill was killed in the 1963 session. He did not explain his comparison.

"No state in the nation," said Sen. Harvey Schwendiman, R-Fremont, "is so well known for one product as is Idaho for its potatoes. The words are synonymous—Idaho and potatoes."

He said the potato industry, including growing and processing, is the state's fastest growing one and more people depend on it than on any other one industry.

Sen. Lloyd Barron, R-Camas, was principal spokesman for the repeal bill. He said it was discrimination to single out the potato industry for free advertising on the license plates.

Sen. Fred Glenn, D-Adams, agreed, saying that livestock, mining, lumbering, recreation and wheat growing should have equal consideration.

But Sen. R. H. Young, R-Canyon, said removal of the "Famous Potatoes" slogan would be "extremely foolish" and Sen. William J. Dee, D-Idaho, said he "heard of Idaho potatoes long before I knew there was a State of Idaho."

All advertising on license plates would have been prohibited under terms of the bill.

Controversy over the "famous potatoes" slogan began early in the session when the Janss Corp. new owner of Sun Valley, suggested license plates should advertise the state's tourist attractions.

Immediate protest was led by potato growers.

* * * * * *

☆ BOISE (AP) — The Idaho House of Representatives ordered on Friday printing of a bill that sponsor Don Pieper, R-Bonneville, said would bring the state $1 million in additional taxes.

Pieper said the measure would substitute a "mathematical formula for the judgment of the tax collector" in determining incomes of Idaho corporations doing business both inside and outside the state.

The House overruled its Printing Committee, which decided not to print the measure because "it was a revenue raising bill and should properly originate in the Revenue and Taxation Committee."

Pieper asked the House to overrule the Printing Committee, which it did by a standing vote.

Under Pieper's formula, corporations would pay Idaho taxes on 65 per cent of their net federal taxable income, unless they could prove by direct accounting methods that their income derived in the state was less than that figure.

Agreement Reached

The House and Senate Education committees reported agreement on a formula for distributing state school funds and began drafting it in bill form.

Individual contributions

DEL LOWE was senior and managing partner of the accounting firm Lowe, Viehweig, Hill, and Gross, one of the outstanding accounting firms in Idaho. For a long time he had been interested in Idaho tax reform, believing it was crucial for the future growth of the state.

CHUCK MCDEVITT was elected to the legislature from Ada County in 1962. His principal interest was in tax reform, which would enable adequate appropriations for public education. He sought out Lowe before the 37th Session of the legislature. Their discussions about the possibility of tax reform and sales tax as being a principal ingredient of that reform quickly led to another individual.

PHIL PETERSON, a professor at the University of Idaho College of Law, also practiced tax law in Lewiston. Like Lowe, Peterson had long felt that significant tax reform had to occur in the state to enable future growth. These individuals agreed to go to work prior to the 37th Session on attempting to create a tax reform package.

There was little data for a foundation or database of financial information that would enable estimates of funds that would be created by individual tax reform or funds that would be lost by the elimination of certain taxes. Lowe went to work creating such a database, obtaining all of the information that existed from the many sources in Idaho—including retail merchants, the Tax Commission, the University of Idaho, Idaho State University, the Department of Commerce—and data from private sources to which Lowe had access.

Peterson began analyzing sales tax laws from various states, obtaining ideas and beginning to draft what could be a sales and use tax for Idaho. The three individuals met at least once a week, typically on Saturday, when approximately half a day was dedicated to reviewing what progress they had made and review of specifics that ultimately went into the tax reform package.

Post-session activity

Several years after the 38th Session, the Lowe, Viehweig, Hill, and Grow firm was acquired by Touche Ross, one of the "Big Eight" firms in the United States that during this period were busy acquiring regional accounting firms. Not long after the acquisition, Touche Ross discovered the asset that it had in Lowe and promptly moved him to be involved on the national level. He became one of the leading bond experts in the country and for a number of years served on the executive committee of Touche Ross. Del died in 2015.

After the 38th Session, Phil Peterson continued to consult with the Idaho legislature on tax matters for a number of years. His tax practice blossomed, and he provided tax analysis and tax programs for several of the most affluent members of the Idaho community.

It was a godsend to the legislature and to Idaho that the two great minds embodied in the persons of Del Lowe and Phil Peterson were available and more than willing to provide their talents to the creation of the tax reform that became a reality in the 38th Session.

In early 1960, Janie McCleary, wife of Jim McCleary, an executive vice president of the Morrison-Knudsen Company, both of whom had long been significant contributors to and fund raisers for the Republican Party and its candidates in Idaho, decided that it was time to organize the Republican Party in Ada County; what organization existed was in disrepair. Janie was a tireless worker and in a few years created an organization that in large measure continues to this day. She attended almost every daily session of the 38th Legislature, and if "her delegation" (Ada County) needed anything in the form of research or additional information, she would find who could provide it and respond quickly.

One of the persons Janie had partnered with on the political basis was Gwen Barnett. Barnett was the daughter of an Oklahoma family that had been active in Republican politics in Oklahoma for a number of years. She had witnessed politics and its goings on in her home as a child and was quite familiar with the processes of politics. She had moved to Idaho with her husband, Steele Barnett, who had come to take a position as a mid-level executive with the then growing Boise Cascade Corporation.

Barnett's interest was in women's political organizations, and she set out to assist community after community in organizing and maintaining a women's Republican group. She tirelessly traveled to communities throughout the state. It seemed no town was too small to catch Barnett's attention and help if there was interest in the creation of a Republican women's organization. In a few short years, Barnett's efforts had brought into existence a political base in the form of these women's organizations.

In mid-1960, Barnett was elected national committeewoman for the Idaho Republican Party. In that role, she became a friend of Dean Burch, then the chairman of the Republican National Committee—appointed by Barry Goldwater.

Barnett would frequent the legislature to offer and provide assistance and, at the request of given legislators, inform her women's groups of actions being taken in their areas.

Following the 1964 presidential election, in which Lyndon Baines Johnson delivered a landslide defeat to Barry Goldwater, a few moderate Republican governors across the country sought Burch's removal.

Uncharacteristically at this time, Governor Smylie, who had always been extremely careful and kept his political head down, agreed to lead and be spokesperson for those moderate governors seeking Burch's removal.

The chairman's position was settled by an agreement among Goldwater, New York governor Nelson Rockefeller, and Burch; accordingly, Ray Bliss, chair of the Ohio Republican Party, was elected.

Following this settlement, Dean Burch sent Smylie a bitter, angry letter that was circulated among Idaho party leaders.

In all probability, Gwen Barnett shared the views of her friend Dean Burch.

And whether it was this action, or some other affront that Barnett had suffered at the hands of Smylie, is not known; but Barnett publicly committed to terminating the political life of Idaho's Republican governor. In 1965, she sought a candidate to oppose Smylie in the Republican primary the next year. She first approached Allan Shepard, who had been a state legislator and was then attorney general. Shepard declined the entreaty and later was appointed to the Idaho Supreme Court.

DON SAMUELSON
BONNER

Barnett then sought out Don Samuelson, a senator from Bonner County. Samuelson, an anti-sales tax senator in the 38th Session, had sustained himself and his family by selling mining and other heavy equipment while traveling in his pickup throughout Idaho, Montana, and eastern Washington. Samuelson was a likable individual and was much more conservative than Smylie was in his tenure as governor. Samuelson agreed to run against Smylie in the 1966 Republican primary

The primary demonstrated just how powerful a political base Barnett had created in the women's organizations in Idaho. That, combined with individuals who opposed Smylie for personal reasons, was enough to defeat him. Samuelson went on to be elected and was a one-term governor.

Barnett had achieved her stated ambition to terminate the political life of Robert E. Smylie. Shortly thereafter, she left her husband and, together with a North Idaho political operative with whom she had become friends, left Idaho.

Outstanding individuals

A number of individuals, legislators and others, made specific contributions during the session.

JOHN CORLETT

Politically Speaking

cent
will
the
for

ch of
Lin-
Ada,
Ada,
gers,
son;

low,
son,

As one looks back at the start of the regular 38th Legislature, now adjourned but continuing in extraordinary session, some of the politics, the power plays and the issues that arose in its 14 overtime days were not in evidence.

each other's actions will be forgotten.

The senators, for example, were prone to blame Rep. Herman McDevitt, D-Bannock, for keeping the legislature in much of its overtime period. McDevitt

JOHN CORLETT, political columnist for the *Idaho Daily Statesman*, had observed the sessions of the Idaho legislature on a daily basis since 1937, and he did so once more in 1965. He had keen insight and the solid trust of politicians as well as the general public.

Corlett was the recipient of a good deal of information that was not available to most newspapers' columnists. He wrote a daily column for the *Statesman* that pretty accurately covered what transpired in any given day on the floor of the legislature as well as an analysis of what was happening, what was going to happen, and what had happened in the past.

Corlett could, from his great memory bank, provide you details as to given individuals in most previous sessions of the legislature and was a valuable resource. He was an individual whom politicians trusted enough to disclose actions they thought they would undertake and to get his opinion on their probable success.

Corlett's presence daily, observing what was going on and making notes, also had the effect of tempering what might have been more tumultuous affairs.

Corlett clearly was a part of the 38th Session of the Idaho legislature.

J.V. Posnick - Shoshone

JOHN V. POSNICK (SHOSHONE), Representative from Shoshone County, operated the largest saloon in Shoshone County and—characteristic of a person in such a position—was a skilled storyteller, able to relay from memory countless tales of historic North Idaho as well as jokes both ribald and not. John was probably in closer contact with many of his constituents than most Representatives were, as in his occupation he saw many of them on a reoccurring basis in any given year.

The one unusual talent he possessed was an encyclopedic knowledge of baseball trivia. A number of baseball fans in the legislature tried again and again to stump John with a question about some little-known baseball fact. No one was successful in stumping John, however.

John was an eager legislator. He worked hard and was an able representative of his constituents.

W.C.Sutton-Washington

W. C. SUTTON (WASHINGTON), a member of the House, was opposed to any and all tax increases or other changes in the status quo as he knew it. He would rise on most occasions to explain that the measure he was opposing would be the one that would destroy a chicken-and-egg business his wife ran to help the family subsist in their difficult labors. After several such laments, Herman McDevitt with the aid of some of his associates examined the state's tax rules and the personal-property tax rules of Washington County for the previous several years. McDevitt then rose on the House floor to announce that, having examined the tax rules of Washington County, there was not a single chicken in Washington County in those tax rules. Unaffected by this revelation, Sutton again rose the following day to oppose a measure whose effect would be, he said, to destroy the chicken-and-egg business that his wife ran.

Ed Williams - Nez Perce

ED WILLIAMS (NEZ PERCE) was a capable, outgoing Representative who was a diligent worker and ably represented Nez Perce County. A schoolteacher and coach, Williams was especially effective on the manner of finance for schools and overall education legislation. A friend of Cecil Andrus, he later became a very significant factor in Andrus' election as governor of Idaho. His very early death by drowning in the Snake River deprived Idaho of a future leader of great promise.

J.L. Palmer-Oneida

JENKINS W. (JENKS) PALMER (ONEIDA), a veteran legislator, was in the 38th Session chair of the House Appropriations Committee, which in connection with the Senate Finance Committee drafted the appropriations bills funding the operation of state government for the next biennium. Palmer had opposed the sales tax and most significant increases in appropriations but had, when the die was cast, done a masterful job with his committee. In the last days of the session, he brought to the floor of the House a bill that would appropriate money to purchase land in the Dry Creek area just west of the then city limits of Boise. This measure was defeated due significantly to the vehement opposition by the Ada County delegation. Upon defeat of this legislation, Palmer rose on the floor of the House and described the Ada County delegation as a "rat pack" that had acted in unison throughout the legislative session.

The following morning, Janie McCleary, then chair of the Ada County Republican Central Committee, presented each member of the Ada County delegation with a gold-plated rat pin, which the delegation wore with pride for the balance of the session.

GENE BUSH (BONNEVILLE).was an Idaho Falls lawyer, highly regarded in his profession and his community. A freshman in the 38th Session, he came to the legislature with a desire to enact legislation that would provide statewide uniformity in property evaluations.

E.L.Bush-Bonneville

Bush worked hard and competently at the drafting of this legislation and in creating the support necessary for its passing.

Opposition to the legislation proposed by Bush and this group was based on the opposition to the valuation of residential property under that measure. Enough opposition was mounted to put the bill on general orders for amendment, but Bush's competent management defeated the amendments proposed and the bill was enacted.

Subsequent legal attacks on the law and its treatment of residential real property saw the Idaho Supreme Court declare that element unconstitutional. The balance of the measure, however, established criteria upon which long sought statewide uniformity was achieved in property evaluations.

James W. Monroe - Nez Perce

JAMES MONROE (NEZ PERCE) was Assistant Minority Leader. In the last session in which the Democrats held a majority of the House, he served as chairman of Revenue and Taxation.

Jim was quite knowledgeable about the operation of the existing tax system and studied any changes sought. Based upon his constituency in Lewiston, Jim felt that the businesses there would suffer if Idaho adopted a sales tax, thus reducing if not eliminating the advantage Idaho businesses had by not having a sales tax and in their minds attracting business from across the Snake River in Clarkston. Jim was one of the leaders of the opposition to the sales tax in the House of Representatives. A student of all bills brought forward, he focused mainly on those that would adversely affect his constituency, which resulted in his opposing all the tax measures proposed during the 38th Session as well as ably representing the Port Authority of Lewiston in seeking additional capacity to finance its operation.

D.V. Manning-Bannock

DARRELL V. MANNING (BANNOCK) was the House Minority Leader in the 38th Session. He had a calm demeanor and an active intellect. Darrell was a pilot and a member of an active Air Force Reserve unit until 1972, when he became a member of the Air National Guard. He also was a student of the rules of the legislature.

Darrell was capable of seeing past the politics of an issue and dwelling on its non-political or apolitical attributes. With Manning as Minority Leader and Bill Lanting as Majority Leader, issues were based not on politics but really on the issues themselves.

As a result, most of the legislation of the 38th Session was bipartisan in nature and represented a division more based on age, occupation, or residence.

Unknown to most of the members of the Legislature, but clearly known and understood by the Speaker, Pete Cenarrusa (a former Marine fighter pilot), on a number of weekends during the 38th Session Manning was unavailable. Cenarrusa never scheduled any significant legislation for Monday in these weeks but dealt mainly with house-keeping measures. Manning always showed up Monday even though on Friday evening he had been taken by jet to Hill Air Force Base in Ogden, Utah. From Ogden, Manning, as Pilot in Command, would take off in an engine-heavy aircraft on a training mission for other pilots and crews who would later fly to Vietnam or some other strategic location. In 1965 the Air Force had received a new aircraft, and these training missions were critical.

Manning later became director of the Idaho Department of Aeronautics, director of the Idaho Department of Transportation, and Adjutant General of the Idaho National Guard. Under Manning's command, many of the state's facilities for aircraft and armor repair were commissioned and built. As Adjutant General, he oversaw construction of the armor-training course in the desert along with maintenance facilities; units trained on that course were important in the two incursions by the U.S. into Iraq and Afghanistan.

ARVIL MILLAR (BINGHAM), a veteran legislator, was the chair of the House Revenue and Taxation Committee. Millar, a farmer near Blackfoot, was keenly aware of Idaho's dire financial straits as it attempted to provide required services with limited funds and a tax structure that provided no real growth.

Arvil Millar - Bingham

As a result, over time he had become an advocate of the sales and use tax as the only way to provide for the essential funds to operate the state government and provide added revenue as the population and financial wellbeing of the state itself prospered. Millar was a prime factor in the passage of the sales and use tax in the 38th Session as well as the accompanying legislation necessary to make the sales tax effective and workable.

He was the fourth chair of Rev and Tax in modern times to have proposed a sales and use tax and the first to accomplish its passage. Under Millar, the Rev and Tax Committee of the 38th Session accomplished more tax revision and updates than any other such committee had accomplished in a session.

W. J. Lanting-Twin Falls

WILLIAM J. LANTING (TWIN FALLS) was a prominent Magic Valley farmer and rancher who served 16 years in the Legislature, beginning in 1959.

He rose to Republican Majority Leader and was House Speaker from 1969 through 1974. He also served on the Idaho Water Resource Board from March 1985 thru March 1989. Lanting is a member of the Idaho and Magic Valley Cattlemen's Associations and the Southern Idaho Livestock Hall of Fame. He was vice chair of the governing board of the Council of State Governments and chairman of the Western Conference of the Council of State Governments.

Helen McKinney - Lemhi

HELEN MCKINNEY (LEMHI) came to the legislature from Salmon. She had a quick wit and was a fast study. She immersed herself in the legislative process and then began personally making friends among her fellow legislators. Helen did her homework, attended committee meetings, and as a result was able to have her point of view reflected in several of the bills passed in the 38th Session. Not long after its adjournment, she moved to Canyon County, where she established herself as one of the leaders of the Republican Party for more than thirty years,

V. Ravenscroft-Gooding

VERN RAVENSCROFT
(GOODING) had as his principal and seemingly sole interest in the 38th Session was the devising and passage of legislation that would distribute state funding among the school districts in Idaho, incorporating elements of attendance, taxing ability of the various districts, and population of the districts. This was a challenging task in that each Representative tended to look at the legislation through the eyes of his or her own districts. Were they going to gain or lose because of this legislation? As a rule, the more populous school districts were going to help fund those smaller school districts. Ravenscroft accomplished this task, although it took several amendments to the initial proposals to gain the support required for passage. Sometime following this session, Vern changed political parties and over the next number of years was a candidate for governor on the Republican ticket.

H.D. Summers-Ada

H. DEAN SUMMERS (ADA) thoroughly enjoyed the legislative process. The 38th was his second Session. Dean had management and ownership experience in the commercial paper business and as an insurance agent. In these fields, he had significant knowledge and practical experience in these fields that he brought to bear on legislation that was adopted.

As a member of the Ada County delegation, he also was instrumental in the granting of four-year-degree status to Boise Junior College, the sales and use tax, and other significant 38th-Session legislative accomplishments. Dean served additional terms in the House of Representatives and as a senator from Ada County.

His knowledge and expertise are reflected in a good deal of existing law in Idaho and in the fields of insurance and commercial paper.

E.Johnson - Franklin

ELLIS JOHNSON (FRANKLIN) was a pharmacist in Preston; he and his brother Paul owned the local pharmacy. Ellis' jovial demeanor cleverly disguised the keen mind and determination to accomplish those things that Ellis thought were in the best interests of Idaho. Those faculties had clearly served him as an officer in the United States Marine Corps.

Ellis had a million stories and told them with great glee. He often bragged that he and Paul through their "cough medicine" distributed more alcohol in Franklin County than did the State Liquor Dispensary. You had to be careful in speaking with Ellis, because his easy demeanor rather than the substance of what he was talking about would attract your attention. At the end of the conversation, when he said "well, are you with me on that?" you could easily say yes, not fully understanding to what you had committed yourself.

Ellis was firm in his commitment to education and his desire to see education in Idaho adequately funded so that it might move forward.

Don Pieper-Bonneville

DON PIEPER (BONNEVILLE) was an Idaho Falls businessman who was a distributor of petroleum products and the retail sales of the same at some locations in eastern Idaho.

Pieper was a capable legislator. He did his homework, especially in those matters of particular interest to him.

He had an analytical mind that led him to a number of conclusions that he demonstrated were well based; after some time in politics, he concluded that Thursday, was the "slow news day." As a result, often late in the afternoon on a Thursday, Don would rise on the floor on a matter of personal privilege and make a speech on some issue that dealt with the legislative process or with the manner in which the legislature was addressing issues that Pieper either supported or opposed. Whatever the topic, Pieper almost always ended up with a news article about his statements, not only in his hometown but in Boise and North Idaho as well.

Pieper had been mentioned by many as a gubernatorial candidate and would have run had not the Democrats nominated Cecil Andrus, who proved to be extremely popular.

O. Hansen-Bonneville

ORVAL HANSEN (BONNEVILLE), raised on a farm near Idaho Falls, was awarded a Rotary Foundation Fellowship following his undergraduate work at the University of Idaho. He received an advanced degree from the London School of Economics and a law degree from George Washington University. Hansen worked with Bush on real property tax equalization through legislation. A strong supporter of education, he also supported tax reform.

Hansen was elected Idaho's Second District U.S. Congressman and through that became involved in nuclear energy issues. The Atomic Energy Commission took over the Arco Desert Naval Gun Range and its facilities. Hansen became a close friend of Dixie Lee Ray, chair of the Atomic Energy Commission. After he lost the Republican congressional primary in 1974, he remained in Washington, D.C., as, among other things, a prominent member of the nuclear industry legal community.

M.D. Parsley - Bonner

MERLE PARSLEY (BONNER) came to Boise as a North Idaho legislator, and he was mentored by Herman McDevitt. Parsley loved Boise and became a student of state government and its operations. Parsley moved his family to Boise, and he and his wife opened a sandwich-and-snack facility primarily serving public school students. The shop became a "North End" Boise icon. Parsley was appointed director of the State Insurance Fund by Governor Cecil Andrus. He proved to be a very successful manager of the Fund and was able to distribute annual dividends to State Insurance rate-payers.

RAY W. RIGBY
MADISON

RAY RIGBY(MADISON) was a freshman senator in the 38th Session. He was a staunch supporter of public education and understood the monetary needs thereof. This led him to be an early supporter of sales tax and tax reform.

Rigby was a quick study and a hard worker and quickly became the one to go to for eastern Idaho support. John Corlett named Rigby the outstanding freshman senator of the 38th Session.

Rigby remained a political force for decades, deeply involved in water litigation critical to Eastern Idaho.

HERMAN MCDEVITT
(BANNOCK) was first elected to the legislature when he was still a law student at the University of Idaho College of Law; he was granted an excuse from classes during the legislative session, but he had to return at the end of the session and pass all of the examinations and other requirements as though he had not served in the legislature.

H.J. McDevitt - Bannock

At the time of the 38th Session, he had already served five terms in the House.

McDevitt was an expert at House rules and parliamentary procedure. He had previously served as Minority Leader but stepped down from that position so that he could be freer to take such action on the floor of the House as he deemed appropriate. McDevitt and Darrell Manning were close personal friends and together could demonstrate the mastery of the rules and procedure that was unequaled.

John Corlett reflected on the tactics of McDevitt on the tax reform maneuvering: "McDevitt Bannock did conduct a two day slow down, but he was smart enough to do it at a crucial time and perchance may take credit for forcing the Senate to pass the Sales Tax."

In the years after the 38th Session, McDevitt served on the board of directors of the State Water Board; as a commissioner of the Idaho State Parks and Recreation Department, and on the Western States Water Policy Council and was subsequently appointed by President Gerald R. Ford Idaho's representative to the Pacific Fisheries Management Council; he was elected chairman of that organization by its membership. McDevitt served as a member of the negotiating team of the Pacific Fisheries Management Council and was an active participant in negotiating with Japanese, Taiwanese, and other countries engaged in fishing in the North Pacific and Bering Sea to set limits on specific species catches.

McDevitt had been appointed even though the then governor, Cecil Andrus, had recommended another individual; McDevitt's reputation and experience as a conservationist and negotiator had obviously been called to the attention of the president.

PERRY SWISHER
BANNOCK

PERRY SWISHER
(BANNOCK) had been a political figure in Idaho politics for many years prior to the 38th Session; he had served on the interim tax committee that had held hearings throughout the state in the 1950s, then concluded that the state "needed tax reform," and specifically recommended the adoption of a sales and use tax.

Swisher carried the sales and use tax measure on the floor of the Senate in both the 37th and 38th Sessions. On each occasion, he was masterful in his presentation and drew applause from opponents as well as supporters of the sales tax proposal.

He went on to be a very active member of the Idaho Public Utilities Commission, setting rates for utilities; during his tenure on the PUC, it was an active commission, inquiring into the reason for rates and rate increases requested to an extent that had not been seen in a number of years.

After the 38th Session, Swisher made a disappointing run for governor, but he remained very active as a political figure through writing a column in several daily newspapers and for a time being editor of a weekly news publication himself.

Swisher was featured several times by major publications in Idaho and in the West based on his colorful career in politics and as a journalist.

WILLIAM C. RODEN
ADA

WILLIAM C. (BILL) RODEN (ADA) was the sole senator from Ada County in the 38th Session, the last before reapportionment. The burden thus fell on him to shoulder legislation directly affecting Ada County. Roden was masterful in his handling of matters in the Senate, successfully maneuvering the Boise Junior College legislation and all of the technical tax reform bills that were companion to the sales and use tax bill through the Senate. He remained in the Senate for a number of years and remained popular and effective in that body.

After Roden's departure from service in the Senate, his law practice more and more took on representing clients in dealing with the state and with legislation that directly affected them. As the State grew, this aspect of his law practice also grew to the extent that for many years, Roden has been listed by many publications as the leading and most effective lobbyist in Idaho.

If there was an important piece of legislation being addressed, you could feel certain that Bill Roden and one or more of his clients were involved.

HAROLD L. RYAN
WASHINGTON

HAROLD A. (HAL) RYAN
(WASHINGTON) was an engaging, effective lawyer practicing law in Weiser, Idaho.

Well-liked by fellow members of the Senate, Ryan was an effective senator in the 38th Session, but he was weighed down by one significant problem: his constituents were persuaded that if a sales and use tax were to pass, all of the business in the town of Weiser would flow across the Snake River to Oregon, where business would flourish to the detriment of the Idaho counties bordering Oregon. His constituency insisted that to prevent the passage of a sales and use tax, either an alternative tax or a reduced budget would be necessary. Ryan's legislative activities therefore were mostly negative, although he and several of his associates did propose alternate tax measures.

Following the 38th Session, Ryan was appointed by the President of the United States to serve as the federal district judge for the District of Idaho. Ryan was a competent and well liked federal district judge.

ARTHUR P. MURPHY
SHOSHONE

ART MURPHY (SHOSHONE) was one of the seniors in terms of tenure in the Senate. Although a Democrat and often in the minority, he was extremely effective in passing legislation that he deemed favorable to his constituency and opposing that which he considered unfavorable.

To many, Art Murphy was "Mr. Democrat." If someone wanted to know if there was a "Democrat position" on any issue and what that that position was or could be, Art Murphy was the person they usually sought out. Murphy was intelligent, congenial, outgoing.

If you didn't like Art Murphy, it was probably your fault.

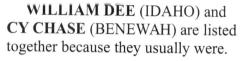

WILLIAM J. DEE
IDAHO - MINORITY LEADER

C. C "CY" CHASE
BENEWAH

WILLIAM DEE (IDAHO) and **CY CHASE** (BENEWAH) are listed together because they usually were.

Today, they probably would be labeled "Libertarian." In the 38th Session, they were pretty much labeled "againsters."

They were opposed to any tax reform; deadly opposed to the sales and use tax; would reduce the budget if they could; and would never consider any increase.

They were both intelligent and usually effective in gathering people to their cause as they opposed the sales tax.

They opposed any funding increase for state education; they opposed four-year status for Boise Junior College.

Dee was a lawyer and Chase a car dealer, and they were leaders of the opposition to the referendum on the sales and use tax and related legislation to be voted on by the public in the 1966 election.

JAMES A. MCCLURE

JAMES A. MᶜCLURE
PAYETTE - ASST. MAJORITY LEADER

JAMES A. MCCLURE (PAYETTE), a very popular and effective lawyer in southwest Idaho, bore the same burden as his friend and associate Hal Ryan in that he represented a county that bordered Oregon; that was a business center for the area that it served; and whose citizens were persuaded that the passage of the sales and use tax by Idaho, when Oregon had none, would result in all of the business and commerce presently engaged in Payette and surrounding counties flowing across the Snake River to Ontario, Oregon, which would become a metropolis. All at the expense of Idaho's bordering counties.

Like his counterpart in Washington County, McClure had to do all in his power to either defeat any sales and use tax proposal or succeed in passing an alternate tax or maintaining a low Idaho budget; the view of McClure by many during this session therefore was one of negativism.

Shortly after the 38th Session, a vacancy occurred in the First Congressional District for the United States House of Representatives, in which Payette County was situated. (This vacancy occurred when the Republican nominee, John Mattmiller, died in the crash of the private plane that he was piloting.) McClure ran and was elected.

When, in 1972, Len Jordan of Idaho retired from the United States Senate, McClure ran and was elected. In the United States Senate McClure was extremely popular, although a Republican he served in the minority most of his tenure.

When Republicans were in the majority, McClure chaired the Senate Committee on Energy and Natural Resources, and he was regarded by all as a most effective United States Senator.

McClure served until he decided to retire, and—unlike many individuals from Idaho who went to Washington—he came home, where he remained extremely popular and where his advice was sought by many on multiple issues.

Robert C. Huntley-Bannock

ROBERT HUNTLEY
(BANNOCK), a freshman legislator in the 38th Session, established a reputation as having a quick mind and being a diligent worker. He was active on a number of issues, and education was of great importance to him.

He continued to pursue litigation to establish constitutional standards for public education and is still engaged in that undertaking, practicing law in Boise after retiring from the Idaho Supreme Court.

Phil Batt- Canyon

PHIL BATT (CANYON), A freshman in the 38th session, he was quickly recognized for his humor and straight forward demeanor which provided him with the ability to create bipartisan alliances and get meaningful legislation adopted.

He served as a Canyon County Representative from 1965-67 and then went on to serve as that county's elected Senator for 12 years (1967-1979.) After which he was elected as the state's 35th Lieutenant Governor from 1979 to 1983.

In 1994, he beat democrat Larry Echohawk to finally break the 24-year democrat stronghold on the Idaho governor's office. During his term of office, he was a strong human rights advocate. He is best remembered for his work in negotiating a legal contract with the US Department of Energy requiring nuclear waste cleanup at the INEL site.

CECIL D. ANDRUS
CLEARWATER

CECIL ANDRUS (CLEARWATER) has a well documented political history, but little has dealt with Andrus as a young senator in the 38th Session.

Andrus was a senator from Clearwater County, whose county seat is Orofino. It is one of the less populated counties in Idaho. It is, as you might guess, on the Clearwater River and had been a part of a group of counties that had voted similarly if not the same on most key issues for a number of years.

A very powerful political operative in Nez Perce County (Lewiston) over the years had helped maintain the block that consisted of the counties of the Clearwater drainage and a few surrounding that area. The pressure on a young senator from Clearwater County to maintain the unity that was expected of him must have been tremendous.

However, when it came to the issue of the sales and use tax and its related legislation, which clearly would be used to raise money in significant fashion to fund K-12 education in Idaho, Andrus saw the need of the education system and the effect that should result from the added financing available through tax reform. He had the courage to break ranks on this issue with other North Idaho senators and support the sales tax measure.

As is well documented, Andrus went on to become an extremely popular governor, serving four terms, and also served as United States Secretary of the Interior.

Sidelook at Slowdown

Filibuster by McDevu
Starts Record-Search

The lengthy filibuster started in the House Wednesday by Rep. Herman McDevitt, D-Bannock, because of his protest that some senators were trying to interfere with House business brought varied actions and reactions from his colleagues.

Veteran legislators and newsmen said the slowdown was one of the longest in recent history — exceeded only by one in the 1946 session which continued until 3 a.m.

Speaker Refuses to Panic

Speaker of the House, Rep. Pete T. Cenarrusa, R-Blaine, said, "I'm not going to panic over this. We will continue to conduct our business in an orderly manner. These things have a way of working themselves out."

Follows Words, Has Substitute

As the clerks took turns reading bills, McDevitt followed their words by checking copies of the bills before him. Once when he thought he noted an error, he called for an explanation from Rep. Larry Mills, R-Ada, speaker pro tempore.

When McDevitt left the floor for a smoke or to consult with someone he was replaced by Rep. Darrell Manning, D-Bannock, minority leader, who watched as the bills were read. Rep. Merle Parsley, D-Bonner, was "substituted" at another time.

Rule 70, which disallows smoking on the floor, was suspended for a period in the morning. In the afternoon, however, each attempt to lift the rule was beaten down.

Once when it was objected to, Rep. Don Peyer, D-Bonneville, said, "I agree with the objector. The rule should not be lifted when the gallery is full." There were less than 10 persons in the gallery at the time.

They Doze, Play Cards, Read

As the reading of bills continued several legislators retired to the coffee room. One promptly took off his coat, stretched out on a table and fell asleep. Others started a card game and a few read newspapers.

'Even Children Throw Tantrums'

At one time when he had the floor, the instigator of the slowdown said, "Nobody promised us anything when we voted on the sales tax." He also objected to the House having to have its legislation passed "bit by bit" and "piece by piece" in the Senate while the upper chamber toyed with the sales tax. And noting the legislature was in its sixth overtime day, he said, "The way I view it we should have been done days ago."

"These children will throw tantrums continuously if they know they will get their way," McDevitt said.

Some Couldn't Savvy Buttons

From time to time representatives would question whether a quorum was on the floor. Then it would be necessary for the speaker to take a tabulation of those present. As the warning bell sounded, legislators appeared from behind the curtains, from the coffee room and from the rotunda. Around 4:30 p.m. when one roll call was taken several of the members apparently were confused because they pushed aye and nay buttons instead of the one indicating present.

Senator Offers Own Opinion

The majority leader of the Senate, George Blick, R-Twin Falls, said about the filibuster that "the House runs their business and we run ours. We are just going to continue our responsibilities by whittling away at the calendar and perform the tasks we were sent here for. When we get our bills passed we may have to go over and investigate."

Gals Serve as Ears for 38th Idaho Legislature

THESE ARE THE GIRLS whose services are a big help to the 38th session of the Idaho Legislature. They "man" the telephone center, provided by Mountain States Telephone Company, to keep legislators in touch with the rest of Idaho. Left to right, standing, are Eileen Chaney, chief operator; Vivian Duke, Bev Cline, Mary Mize and Marie Bischoff. Seated, left to right, are Pat Celeski and Betty Jo Henderlider.

The 38th Idaho legislature had no internet or I-phones to aid them in their daily pursuits. Instead, they depended on hand delivered messages by the ladies who operated the specially installed, statehouse Mountain States telephone message center.

Ongoing public service

A substantial number of members of the 38th Legislative Session continued in their lives to make meaningful commitments to public service:

- a future U. S. Secretary of the Interior (Cecil Andrus)

- a future Treasurer of the United States (Mary Brooks)

- a future First District Congressman and subsequently U.S. Senator (James McClure)

- a future Second District Congressman (Orval Hansen)

- a future United States District Judge (Hal Ryan)

- three future governors (Cecil Andrus, Phil Batt, and Don Samuelson)

- a future Secretary of State of Idaho, and longest serving elected state official in the history of Idaho (Pete Cenarrusa)

- a future Chief Justice of the Idaho Supreme Court (Charles McDevitt, Ada)

- a future Justice of the Idaho Supreme Court (Robert Huntley)

- a future Adjutant General of the Idaho National Guard, Director of Transportation, Director of Aeronautics, Budget Director (Darrell Manning)

- a future Idaho Public Utilities Commissioner (Perry Swisher)

- a future Member of the Idaho Water Resources Board (created the first state water plan), member of the Western States Water Policy Council, Idaho Department of Parks and Recreation Director, member and chairman of the Pacific Fishery Management Council (Herman McDevitt)

- a primary force in creation of the Idaho Association of Commerce and Industry and its first director (Pat Harwood)

- medical doctors (Edwards, Adams, and Head)

- a future director of the State Insurance Fund (Merle Parsley).

Key differences between 1963 and 1965

The laws dealing with this wide-ranging tax reform would go into effect July 1, 1965. The key differences between the 1963 failure and the 1965 successful adoption of this tax reform were:

STRONG, POSITIVE PUBLICITY: created by the public exposure generated by the 1963 Legislature during debate on the tax-measure issues. The cumulative effect of the positive public exposure was highly significant.

STRONG LEGISLATIVE ADVOCACY: Representatives and Senators who had supported the tax measure in the 1963 Legislature ran for re-election advocating that measure and the benefits that would accrue to education and local government. All of the candidates who ran supporting tax reform were ultimately returned to office. In addition, several new individuals who favored a sales tax were elected.

STRONG EXECUTIVE ADVOCACY: Governor Smylie actively worked for the passage of the tax reform measures. The Governor of the State of Idaho, as chairman of the Land Board and as chief executive officer, has several instruments to capture legislators' attention and to affect legislative votes. For the first time Governor Smylie was willing to publicly act and use these tools to influence legislators. Several of the votes cast during the 1965 Legislature were starkly different from the 1963 Legislature—the apparent result of some persuasive fine-tuning by the Governor.

Of all of the accomplishments of the 38th Session, tax reform was indeed the most significant.

The sales tax legacy

After skillful craftsmanship, artful vote trading, and extensive debate, the dedicated members of the 38th Idaho legislature created a sound fiscal foundation that has served the state well for more than a half-century.

Enactment of the Idaho sales tax provided the state with a stable, predictable tax base. It became the crucial third leg of Idaho's current so-called three-legged tax structure, providing the balance to relieve the state's complete tax-load reliance on just property and state income taxes.

The reliance on that three-legged tax system served the state well until two major changes occurred. A major shift occurred on August 25, 2006, when the legislature slashed property taxes, forcing public schools to rely more on sales and income taxes. Even before that change, the strong fiscal legacy was seriously threatened by ongoing crusades to "fix it." "Fixing it" has almost always meant eroding its true revenue-raising potential by "updating" it with amendments.

Today, the sales tax is the "quick-fix store." It's where you go for some quick cash to fund a "special need," or to exempt yourself from paying your share of the sales tax so you can use that saved money for your own "special need." The truth is, many of the amendments now sapping the revenue strength of the sales tax have long ago lost their purpose, but they still hang on like some unwelcome relative.

It is estimated that the current sales tax could be reduced back to 3 percent and still greatly increase state revenue, if a serious effort was made to repeal exemptions that are no longer beneficial. This proposal has been raised from time to time, but not with any major success. However, unless action is undertaken soon, the stability of Idaho's tax structure will face some major challenges. The logical positive course of action is a comprehensive review of all sales tax exemptions and possible additions of the service Industries to the tax.

Phasing out non-beneficial sales tax exemptions could at the same time lower the state's tax and greatly increase state revenues. This could best be accomplished by a special non legislative committee composed of tax and economic experts to review current deductions and hear beneficiaries' defense of retaining them. Once that original exemption refinement is accomplished, sales tax exemptions should be reassessed on a regularly established basis, perhaps by the Idaho Tax Commission. That would retain an ongoing balance of the three-legged tax structure.

In the end, unless some remedial action is taken to restore balance to Idaho's tax structure, it might become necessary to save the Idaho sales tax the same way it was originally enacted, by the will of the Idaho people.

REPRESENTATIVES
Idaho State Legislature
38th SESSION - 1965

Pete T. Cenarrusa, Speaker- Blaine

L. Lindburg-Custer   Fred Nelson-Jerome   C.W. Holder-Kootenai   Jack V. Carey-Bonneville   J.V. Fomichk-Shoshone   D.B.Garner-Minidoka   John J. Quinn-Boise

Wm.J.Brauner-Canyon   Fred Bayley-Ada   M.C.Sutton-Washington   M.Davidson-Boundary   W.E.L.Able-Payette   Karl Koch-Elmore   Ward A.Miller-Lincoln

Larry W.Mills-Ada   T.E.Jernell-Bannock   O.Hansen-Bonneville   J.D.Claiborn-Twin Falls   E.L.Bush-Bonneville   Lloyd R.Gibby-Ada   Art Manley-Kootenai

H.J.O'Neill-Bannock   Robert K.Hartley-Bannock   Harold Agee-Ada   Virgil E.Porter-Canyon   K.C.Klingler-Madison   Leon R.Smetson-Canyon   W. Comstock-Bingham

R.Barlow-Bannock   H.D.Summers-Ada   Fred R. Koch-Ada   Don Peper-Bonneville   Tony Nemeth-Idaho   D.V.Manning-Bannock

Helen W.Kenney-Lemhi   Don L.Maynard-Butter   M.J.Billington-Valley   F.W.Hirschi-Bear Lake   A.L.White-Clearwater   F.K. Harwood-Jefferson

105

106

About the author

Charles F. McDevitt (1932-2021), a 1956 graduate of the University of Idaho College of Law and a former Chief Justice of the Idaho Supreme Court, was recognized as one of Idaho's most prestigious members of the Idaho State Bar.

He was the recipient of the Idaho State Bar's Distinguished Lawyer Award and the University of Idaho's Faculty Award of Legal Merit, which recognizes an outstanding legal career that exemplifies integrity, public service, and leadership as a legal practitioner.

His record in the legal profession is equally balanced by his impressive personal contribution of community service, with special emphasis dedicated to the well-being and education of Idaho's youth. His personal commitment ran the gamut from educating youth about the law, with the YMCA Youth

Government Program, to many years on the Boise Parks and Recreation board spearheading creation of the 160-acre Simplot Soccer Fields and, a skateboard park, playgrounds, and 20 acres of youth sports space later named the Charles F. McDevitt Youth Sports Complex.

He was a member of the Idaho Volunteer Lawyers Task Force, American Inns of Court, and the University of Idaho Foundation and served as an Ada County public defender.

In the private sector, he served as general counsel, secretary, and vice president of the Boise Cascade Corporation in the 1960s; as president of Beck Industries, a manufacturing and retailing firm in New York; and later as an executive vice president of the Singer Company.

In 1963 and 1965 he was active in local government, serving as Representative in the Idaho state legislature. It was there that McDevitt made one of his most important, long-lasting contributions to Idaho and to its future. He was one of the key architects of the Idaho sales tax, providing Idaho with a sound fiscal foundation that has provided educational funding for more than half a century. Passage of a major tax system is a herculean task, successful only under highly unique circumstances.

And that is what this book is all about. It is McDevitt's inside story of *The GREAT 38th: 'Idaho's Perfect Political Storm.'*